TUPE: LAW & PRACTICE
A Guide to the TUPE Regulations

Fourth edition

by
Wyn Derbyshire & Stephen Hardy

First published by Spiramus Press, 2006

This fourth edition published February 2014

ISBN 978 1907444 82 1

British Library Cataloguing-in-Publication Data.

A catalogue record for this book is available from the British Library.

Important disclaimer:

This book is only intended for guidance purposes and specific legal advice should always be taken before any course of action is pursued.

Spiramus Press Ltd, 102 Blandford Street, London, W1U 8AG.
Telephone 020 7224 0080
www.spiramus.com

Printed by Grosvenor Press, London, UK

For Jo Whiterod (who first introduced the authors to each other)

PREFACE

The time has come for TUPE to be revised once more, given the cascade of TUPE cases, notably and centrally relating to the service provision change. Consequently, the UK Government after much and detailed consultation, has enacted the Collective Redundancies and the Transfer of Undertakings (Protection of Employment) (Amendment) Regulations 2014 ("2014 TUPE Amendment Regulations"). This marks the next destrination point in TUPE's controversial pathway in UK law, from an unethusiatsic starting point in 1981, staggering to a revolutionary consolidation in 2006, followed by a short-lived technical period leading to the present day. Yet, the Preamble of the TUPE Regualtions reminds us that the purpose of TUPE remains 'to safeguard employees' rights where a change in ownership of a business takes place'.

The latest changes represent not only a further attempt to clarify continuing uncertainties inherent in TUPE but also are intended to reduce the burdens on employers of small enterprises.

This guide continues to provide analysis of TUPE in the light of the new 2014 TUPE Amendment Regulations including:

- the scope to "service provision changes" (i.e. outsourcing/contracting-out and in), as well as clarification of the Regulation 3;
- key changes relating to transfer dismissals and changes to terms and conditions;
- pensions obligations under TUPE;
- clarified 'joint'consultation rights; and
- the confusing application of TUPE where the transferor is insolvent.

Whilst this book, as ever, brings lawyers, politicians and policymakers, HR practitioners, as well as academics, up to speed in this important area, the EU has announced its intention to examine whether another revised Directive is required. This book aims to keep pace with these changes, providing practical advice and cutting edge analysis.

We would like to thank our families, our employers and publisher.

The law is stated as at 31 January 2014.

Wyn Derbyshire and Stephen Hardy

January 2014

CONTENTS

CONTENTS

TABLES OF AUTHORITIES
Cases

TABLES OF AUTHORITIES

TABLES OF AUTHORITIES

Statutes

Regulations

TABLES OF AUTHORITIES

European Directives

GLOSSARY OF TERMS

ACAS	Arbitration, Conciliation & Advisory Service
ARD	Acquired Rights Directive
BIS	Department of Business, Innovation & Skills
CBI	Confederation of British Industry
DTI	Department of Trade & Industry
EAT	Employment Appeal Tribunal
ECJ	European Court of Justice
EHRC	Equality & Human Rights Commission
EOC	Equal Opportunities Commission
EP	European Parliament
EPCA	Employment Protection (Consolidation) Act 1978
ERA	Employment Rights Act 1996
EReLA	Employment Relations Act 1999
ET	Employment Tribunal
ETO	'Economic, Technical & Organisational'
EU	European Union
EWC	European Works Council
IT	Industrial Tribunal
TUC	Trades Union Congress
TULRCA	Trade Union and Labour Relations Act 1992
TUPE	Transfer of Undertakings (Protection of Employment)
TURERA	Trade Union Reform & Employment Rights Act 1993
UK	United Kingdom

1.   TUPE IN CONTEXT

The Transfer of Undertakings (Protection of Employment) Regulations 1981 (TUPE 1981) caused much turmoil between 1982 and 2013; as a result, their importance in employment law and HR practices has become paramount, since for employers 'business transfers' can either mean commercial survival or a symbol of success whereas employees' concerns focus on job security and terms and conditions of their employment. In this guide, we will encounter the inherent conflict of interest between business interests and contractual rights. Notably, given the widespread reorganisation of businesses and the vast application of contracting-out in the UK's public sector since the 1980s, the controversy between employers' business interests and employees' contractual rights has intensified. It is in respect of this conflict that this guide aims to analyse and explain the law relating to business transfers in the UK in order to understand the relevant legal principles and identify good HR practice in this area.

In the chapters comprising this book, the employment rights enshrined in the TUPE legal framework will be examined in Chapter 2, whilst Chapter 3 presents guidance on the key issue of pensions.

Chapter 4 discusses the thorny issue of insolvency and Chapter 5 explains the significance of contracting-out under TUPE's auspices. Against all of this informative legal analysis, the closing chapter provides advice on the 2014TUPE Amendment Regulations. This opening chapter now seeks to provide the necessary background to embark upon this analysis of the law surrounding TUPE.

1.1.   TUPE or not TUPE?

Those involved with employment law or HR will undoubtedly have heard of TUPE. Before TUPE came into force in 1982 in the UK, the established common law provided that in the event of a business transfer, the existing contracts (being personal in nature) were automatically terminated and the employee became redundant (see *Nokes v. Doncaster Amalgamated Collieries Ltd*[1]). TUPE changed this long-standing legal position based on the freedom of contract, replacing it with a law which complied with the EEC's original Acquired Rights Directive 77/187/EEC (the ARD). This Directive was passed to *"safeguard employees' interests in the event that a business in which they work was sold"*. This puts the significance of business transfers

---

[1]Nokes v. Doncaster Amalgamated Colleries Ltd [1940] AC 1014 HL

into its rightful EU context. The law relating to transfers of undertakings, or business transfers as they are more commonly known, has since its advent been a peculiar feature of both English and European Community law, as it ties so many different legal strands together, such as company, commercial, insolvency, and employment law, as well as 'new' questions about the development of EU social policy and the protection of pension rights on business transfers. With hindsight, the law relating to business transfers, due to its multi-faceted nature, can almost be seen as a time bomb, ticking away since 1977, waiting to explode.

Business transfers can take place for several reasons. What is common about business transfers, unlike share transfers, is that they bring about a change in employer. The most common form of business reorganisation in the UK is by the transfer of share capital. These share transfers, as they are known, involve shares in a company becoming the property of another shareholder (or shareholders). In share transfers involving the sale of a company which is also an employer, the identity of the employer remains the same and due to that fact, in the UK, they are distinct from legally protected business transfers. In the circumstances of a share transfer, the employer-employee contractual relationship is unaffected by a share transfer, leaving the employees with the same degree of enforceable contractual rights (and obligations) as they had before the transfer. However, there is no analogy to TUPE in a share transfer providing any "special" degree of protection. Consequently, these share transfers are usually termed 'take-overs', 'mergers' or 'amalgamations'. Although Community law excludes share transfers from the scope of the ARD, some EU Member States have chosen to include them within the scope of their relevant domestic legislation incorporating the ARD requirements, whilst others exclude them. In contrast, business transfers involving the sale or disposition of assets that do result in changes in the identity of the employer are legally regulated by the ARD. This distinction and its effects will be discussed further in the following chapter.

The evolution of UK employment law has since the 1940s demonstrated much legal flexibility towards business transfers, as was aptly described in the *Nokes* case by Lord Atkin, when he referred to: "*...the remarkable legal consequences of the courts [bringing] about this revolution in the law that led to companies being able to shake off the restrictions, only when they are minded to transfer their business to another and probably a larger company*". The importance of the contractual employment relationship, upon which UK employment law is founded, has therefore determined much of the course of UK regulation including the law relating to business transfers.

1.2. The Original (1977) Directive

By 1972, there was an emerging view amongst the heads of government of the Member States that the EU (then EC) should adopt a policy of more rigorous action in the social field. This led to the Social Action Programme which was adopted by the Council of Ministers in 1974. The Social Action Programme produced a series of Directives which were adopted between 1974 and 1979 and which constitute the main body of Community labour law. Amongst these was the ARD which was adopted in 1977. Unlike much of the development of UK employment law, the origins of the ARD derive from European sources.

EU law-making since 1975 has been fundamental in shaping the terms of both individual and collective labour law rights in the UK. As a consequence of this EU regulation, a number of major labour law controversies, particularly those relating to the EU's desire to create a 'Social Europe' has led to the UK adopting an aggressive, anti-European stance when it comes to EU labour law. Closely associated with this EU-UK dispute about the sovereignty of labour law is the law relating to business transfers, established by the fact that the ARD was one of the first pieces of EU labour law that the UK was forced to adopt, having been pursued in infraction proceedings by the EU Commission. Provisions reflecting the ARD were belatedly transposed 'with a lack of enthusiasm' into UK law under the 1981 TUPE Regulations. The ARD, therefore, plays a salient role, both historically and contemporarily, in the debate surrounding the potential development of EU social policy and in explaining the current state of both the EU and UK law governing business transfers. However, in a UK context, the answer to the question, 'why did we need the ARD?', lies in the shortcomings of the common law, as highlighted by the House of Lords' decision in 1940 in *Nokes v. Doncaster Amalgamated Collieries Ltd.*

The common law underlying a contract of employment did not provide for any continuity of employment in respect of any changes in ownership of a business. In the *Nokes* case, the House of Lords held that where a change in the legal corporate personality takes place, normally by the sale of assets comprising a business undertaking, employees' contracts are terminated. The rule in *Nokes* was explicable on the basis of freedom of contract. Subsequently, protective statutory provisions were enacted, in order to establish extra-contractual measures to allow for the preservation of the continuity of employment under s. 218 of ERA 1996. Furthermore, s. 141 of ERA 1996 modified the common law by offering protection to the former employer by prohibiting the right of an employee to claim redundancy if, on a business transfer, the employee refused an offer of suitable alternative employment with the new employer. This prevented employees from complaining about business transfers. Other legal cases, such as *Lloyd v. Brassey[2], Woodhouse v. Peter Brotherhood Ltd[3], Pambakian v. Brentford Nylons Ltd[4] and Melon v. Hector Powe Ltd[5]*, all before the introduction of TUPE, had recognised the inherent weaknesses of the common law relating to transfers and so TUPE was much welcomed.

1.3. The original TUPE Regulations - 1981

In 1981, the UK Parliament convened the political debate, introducing the TUPE Regulations which transposed the controversial ARD into English law (for House of Lords debate see Hansard HL 10.12.1981 col. 1490 and also Hansard HL 17 & 24.7.1986 cols. 1057 and 450 respectively). The Under-Secretary of State for Employment's *"...remarkable lack of enthusiasm"* (See Hansard HC Deb 7.12.1981, col. 680, then David Waddington MP) about these Regulations in emphasising that they were: *"...Community obligation(s) assumed as long ago as 1977 and 1978"* was clearly noted. However, the intentions of the former Labour Administration, which introduced this legislation during its British Presidency of the then European Community, were defended by Harold Walker MP, the then Shadow Employment spokesman. He noted that the delay between 1977 and 1981 was in fact Conservative-made and deliberate, so as to produce a: *"butchered version"* of the ARD. He maintained that the: *"...vague, open-ended, and ill-defined, economic, technical or organisational reasons [used to] dismiss an employee"* would undermine the effectiveness of the legislation.

In fact, such widespread attempted evasion of the TUPE Regulations, either by design or ignorance or confusion, has occurred in practice, as is evident from the numerous cases brought before Tribunals and the Courts. Thus, from this hurried and late enactment, the TUPE Regulations emerged as and have since produced both a political and legal minefield for business transfers. The intensity of the debate is typified by Lord Wedderburn's contribution in the House of Lords' debate on the introduction of the TUPE Regulations in 1981 after he stated that: *"[These Regulations] ...snatch away the rights which were intended by the Directive, like some bicycle thief snatching purses in the night"* (see Hansard HL Deb 10.12.1981, col. 1490).

---

[2] Lloyd v. Brassey [1969] 2 QB 98 CA

[3] Woodhouse v. Peter Brotherhood Ltd [1972] ICR 186 CA

[4] Pambakian v. Brentford Nylons Ltd [1978] ICR 665 EAT

[5] Melon v. Hector Power Ltd [1981] ICR 43 HL

Wedderburn's foresight recognised the numerous drafting loopholes which the anomalies between the 1977 ARD and the TUPE Regulations 1981 created. After nearly two decades of confusion, in 1998 the Amending Directive was agreed and following its consolidation in 2001, the TUPE Regulations 2006 were enacted on 7 February 2006, and came into force on 6 April 2006.

2.   EMPLOYMENT RIGHTS UNDER TUPE

In the last chapter the social, economic and political contexts of the law relating to business transfers were introduced. In this chapter, an examination of the legal provisions underlying the amended ARD 1998 as enforced in the UK under the TUPE Regulations 2006, will be undertaken.

2.1.   1998 ARD

The EU regulation on business transfers seeks to safeguard employees' rights in the event of business reorganizations, so as to ensure (as summarized by the ECJ in *Wendleboe*[1] that: *"... as far as possible, the employment relationship continues unchanged with the transferee and by protecting workers against dismissals motivated solely by the fact of the transfer"*. This text has already observed that the original ARD was enacted in European law in 1977, but was not implemented in UK law until 1982. Following concessions made at the 1998 Cardiff EU Summit, the British Presidency of the EU was able to secure an agreed, amended draft of a revised ARD, which was enacted in late 1998 and led to the TUPE Regulations 2006 which reflect the amended ARD and came into force on 6 April 2006.

Articles 1 and 2 of the amended ARD concern its scope and definitions. Article 1 applies to the transfer of an undertaking, or part of an undertaking, as a result of a legal transfer within the territorial scope of the EU. Article 2 provides the necessary working definitions of the central terms: *'transferor'*, meaning the person who ceases to be the employer; and *'transferee'*, meaning the person who becomes the employer. Article 3 restates the aims of the Directive. The integral purpose of the ARD is that the transferor's rights, obligations and liabilities arising from the contracts of employment with the transferring employees existing on the date of the business transfer are transferred to the transferee and that the transferee shall continue to observe those terms and conditions, collective agreements and any pre-existing trade union recognition. The only exception to this general rule is contained in Article 3(3) which stipulates that such provisions shall not cover employees' rights to old-age, invalidity or survivors' benefits under supplementary company or inter-company pension schemes outside the statutory social security schemes in Member States. The effect of this exception will be discussed more fully in Chapter 3.

---

[1] Wendleboe v. LJ Musik Aps (In Liquidation) [1986] 1 CMLR 316 ECJ

Central to this secondary legislation are Articles 4 to 6 which seek to *safeguard employees' rights*. Article 4 declares that a business transfer cannot result in dismissal or redundancy, except where such dismissals are for economic, technical or organisational (ETO) reasons. Where an employee is dismissed or made redundant prior to a business transfer, then the transferee (i.e. the new employer) shall be regarded as having been responsible for termination of the contract. Article 5 asserts that the primary aim of the ARD is to preserve the employees' rights post-transfer. In terms of consultation, Article 6 requires the parties to the business transfer (the transferor and transferee) to inform and consult their employees, or their recognised unions, giving the reasons for the business transfer, explaining the legal, economic and social implications of the business transfer, as well as the envisaged effects of the transfer on those employees. This consultation must be undertaken *"in good time"*, before the transfer, and *"with a view to seeking agreement"*. These obligations may be restricted to either trade unions only, or alternatively, to individual employees only (these consultation issues will be considered later in this Chapter, in detail).

Articles 7 to 10 involve the *enforcement and implementation* of the Directive. The EU Council addressed the Directive to all Member States, who were obliged to bring these provisions into force within two years and that such national legislation should be registered with the EU Commission once enacted, in order for the EU Commission to submit these to the EU Council for confirmation. The ARD lays down the minimum provisions to be adopted; it does allow EU Member States to introduce laws more favourable to employees than the minimum requirements prescribed by the ARD.

2.2.   UK's Pre-Existing Law before TUPE 1981

As we have already observed, before the ARD, UK common law provided a less sophisticated legal framework and one which was largely based on the freedom of contract. At common law, a business transfer bringing about a change in ownership, resulted in the automatic termination of a contract of employment giving rise to a dismissal which entitled employees to claim wrongful dismissal, a redundancy payment or compensation for unfair dismissal. As Lord Atkin commented in *Nokes*, notwithstanding all of the common law's shortcomings in relation to business transfers: *"...the servant was left with his inalienable right to choose whether he would serve a new master or not"*, meaning that freedom of contract was retained in the employment relationship. A similar decision was reached by the EAT in *Woods v. WM Car Services (Peterborough) Limited*[2]. This case involved the new owners of a business, who, having agreed to continue the employment of employees on their respective existing terms and conditions, later asked all their employees to accept a lower wage and longer hours. One of the employees, Woods, rejected the new terms and was dismissed. The case turned on whether constructive dismissal could be found. The Employment Appeal Tribunal (EAT), agreeing with the Industrial Tribunal (IT), found that constructive dismissal could not be established. The employee's appeal was subsequently dismissed by the Court of Appeal. The TUPE Regulations 1981 did not come into force in the UK until 1982, and this case demonstrates the type of behaviour the ARD was intended to prevent, as Browne-Wilkinson J. suggested in his judgment in *Woods*.

The ARD and TUPE, in a UK context, marked a departure from the rigid common law doctrine of privity of contract, a doctrine which justifies dismissals and imposes no continuity of employment when the ownership of a business changed. The pre-1982 common law is now, of course, superseded by the TUPE Regulations. TUPE has often been criticised for limiting the freedom of employers to arrange both their contractual and commercial affairs as they choose, so as to minimise their employment law liabilities. The remainder of this Chapter will examine those criticisms, by evaluating the current TUPE framework up to April 2006, so as to provide a background to the TUPE Regulations 2006, as well as act as guidance in applying the 2006 Regulations.

2.3. The former TUPE Regulations 1981

From the perspective of the early 1990s and later, employment law is predominantly a statutory subject, set in a common law context, and subject to the vagaries of judicial interpretation, and the main engine of its development has been legislative rather than judicial. In the case of business transfers, a statutory accommodation of the ARD was drafted, implemented and interpreted by the judiciary in the UK. The UK has implemented its obligations arising from the ARD in its TUPE Regulations 1981. These Regulations, which came into force in 1982, aimed to ensure that once a business transfer was proposed, employers would consult and inform employees, as well as provide for the automatic transfer of the contracts of employment of the employees affected by the business transfer. The TUPE Regulations 1981 were supposed to fully implement the

---

[2] Woods v. WM Car Services (Peterborough) Ltd; [1981] ICR 666 EAT

original 1977 ARD, as required under s.2 of the European Communities Act 1972. Subsequently, Regulations 1 to 3 and 10 to 13 came into force on 1 February 1982, whereas Regulations 4 to 9 and 14 came into operation after 1 May 1982. They were amended in 1993 by s. 33 TURERA, in 1995 by the Terms and Conditions of Employment (Collective Redundancies Business Transfers) Regulations and again in 1996 by s. 218 of ERA. These Regulations were further amended in 1999.

Regulation 1 of the TUPE Regulations 1981 allowed those Regulations to be cited and declared the dates when they came into force. Regulation 2(1) established definitions in order to assist the usage of these Regulations. A wide definition of employee is provided, since it includes anyone who works for another, except an independent contractor. The essential term *'undertaking'* is defined as *'any trade or business'*. Originally this excluded any undertaking or part thereof which is not in the nature of a commercial venture, but following TURERA's amendment to Regulation 2(1), an undertaking now includes any non-commercial trade or business. Regulation 2(2) provided for part of an undertaking, including separate, severable or self-contained parts, to be an identifiable part of the business as a whole, so long as the part is recognisable. Despite all of these definitions, the Regulations were limited in scope and they excluded certain types of employment, for example, overseas employments (Regulation 13(1)).

The central concept upon which the Regulations relied upon was that there must be a *'relevant transfer'*, was defined in Regulation 3. This concept was defined as a transfer of undertaking or part of an undertaking situated in the UK (Regulation 2(1)). The EAT in *Premier Motors (Medway) Ltd. v. Total Oil of GB Ltd*[3], held that under the Regulations a transfer was considered the same as a change in the ownership of the business. In contrast, the ECJ's approach indicates a belief that the Directive is more far-reaching and is not limited solely to a change in ownership, and TURERA's amendment to Regulation 3(4) clarifies that a transfer takes place irrespective of whether or not any property is transferred.

The test established in *Kenmir Ltd. v. Frizzell*[4], to determine whether a business is being transferred as a 'going concern', has regard to the substance of the transfer rather than its form, giving consideration to the

---

[3] Premier Motor (Medway) v. Total Oil GB Ltd [1984] 84 CA

[4] Kenmir Ltd. v. Frizzell [1968] 1 WLR 329 CA

whole of the circumstances relating to the transfer. Under the 'going concern' test, the vital question is whether the effect of the business transfer means that the business transferred "could carry on without interruption". This test was approved in *Lloyd v. Brassey*, where Lord Denning MR asked *"Does the business remain the same business but in different hands?"* Similarly, in *Spijkers*[5] the ECJ held that it is necessary to find an 'economic entity' following a transfer for there to be a relevant business transfer. The 'economic entity' test, as it has become known, has been widely applied to several circumstances since 1986. In particular, it was applied in the ECJ's rulings in *Redmond*[6] and *Rask*[7]. Whether or not these tests have been satisfied in any particular set of circumstances remains a question of fact for the Courts and Tribunals to decide. It is worth emphasising that a 'relevant' business transfer applies only to a transfer of undertaking and not a take-over by means of share transfer.

Regulation 4 provided for business transfers by receivers or liquidators. Thus, where an administrator or receiver transfers a company or part of a company's undertaking to a wholly owned subsidiary of the company, this would not be deemed a business transfer until the transferee company ceases to be wholly owned by the transferor, or alternatively, when the relevant undertaking is transferred by the transferee company to another person. Regulation 4 had no such equivalent provision in the ARD. The ECJ has held that the ARD was inapplicable to insolvency. Subsequently, the ECJ held that the ARD can apply in restricted circumstances where the purpose was to protect the assets of the business from the creditors and allow the business to continue trading.

The *Spence*[8] case illustrated the problematical 'prior to transfer' position of the legislation with regard to liquidation. This case involved receivership of a company where the Secretary of State was the custodian because of the liability as prescribed by the redundancy fund. However, once the business was sold, the employees were reemployed. The dispute arose out of the fact that the Secretary of State claimed that the liability was transferred to the transferee under Regulation 5 of the TUPE Regulations 1981 (which specified that transfers to which the TUPE Regulations 1981 applied did

---

[5] Spijkers v. Gebroeders Benedik Abbatoir CV [1986] ECR 119 ECJ

[6] Redmond Stichting v. Bartol & others [1992] IRLR 366 ECJ

[7] Rask & Christenen v. ISS Kantineservice A/s [1993] IRLR 133 ECJ

[8] Secretary of State for Department of Employment v. Spence [1986] 3 WLR 383 CA

not terminate contracts of employees working in the undertaking to be transferred, but rather transferred them so they became contracts between the employees and the transferee). In other words, employment contracts were not automatically terminated as was found in *Nokes*, which had relied on common law principles which the TUPE Regulations 1981 had overruled. The Secretary of State contended that Regulation 5(3) applied Regulation 5(1) to contracts not only existing at the moment of business transfer, but those terminated immediately before, relying upon *Apex Leisure Hire v. Barrat*[9]. The Court of Appeal held that Regulation 5(1) applied, but that a contract which had already been terminated by the transferor could not be terminated again by the business transfer. Subsequently, Regulation 4 was amended in 1987, in order to provide for the preservation of the receiver's or liquidator's freedom as contained in the Insolvency Act 1986, when attempting to sell the business as a 'going concern'; the latter practice being known as 'hiving-off' or 'hiving-down'. The transfer by the receiver or liquidator to the subsidiary company was not to be treated immediately as a 'relevant transfer'. Regulations 4(1)(a) and (b) applied where the ultimate transferee acquired the undertaking by the transfer of shares in the subsidiary company and then, a 'relevant business transfer' emerged. This amended provision solely ensures that the business transfer was actually only suspended.

In respect of receivership, the House of Lords in *Litster*[10], a case involving the dismissal of an entire workforce one hour before going into receivership, held that liability for these dismissals passed to the transferee because these workers were *"employed immediately before the transfer"* under Regulation 5(3). An exception to the general application of the Regulations was to be advanced with regard to insolvency-related business transfers. The ECJ in *Wendleboe v. LJ Musik Aps (In Liquidation)* presented the question whether Article 3(1) of the Directive required EU Member States to enact provisions which would transfer a vendor's obligations to his former employees and those employed at the moment of business transfer? It was held by the ECJ that there was no need for enactment because it was: *"... doubtful whether the Regulations would improve the position of the employees."* The advantages of automatic termination for the transferee were that they would be free of legal obligations and able to re-engage former employees selectively. This selective re-engagement was made illegal by the TUPE

---

[9] Apex Leisure Hire v. Barratt [1984] IRLR 224 EAT

[10] Litster v. Forth Dry Dock & Engineering [1989] ICR 341 HL

Regulations 1981 which provided for the automatic transfer of employees, whilst Regulation 8(1) protected employees from unfair dismissal. However, it should be noted that Regulation 8(2), the 'Economic, Technical and Organisational' (ETO) defences, preserved the employer's freedom to some degree. The decision in *Spence* deprived employees of certain benefits which were conferred by the Regulations, most notably, basic pay as provided for in the redundancy fund, as well as no compensatory award in unfair dismissal claims.

Furthermore, the protection provided to employees by the Court of Appeal in *Berriman v. Delabole Slate Ltd*[11], of the right to constructive dismissal in a transfer situation, was (and is) undercut by ETO defences. *Spence* has often been seen as an unwelcome decision, since the Court of Appeal failed to grasp that if a contract is not transferred, then the liability for terminating it is so transferred by Regulation 5(2). This was highlighted in the *Litster* decision which conflicts with the ECJ in *Wendelboe*. Under Regulation 5(2)(a), the transferee is liable in respect of termination of the contract before dismissal. In *Berriman* the employer's rights to change terms and conditions unilaterally were removed, but this position was restored by *Spence*.

As mentioned above, the effects of a business transfer on contracts of employment in the TUPE Regulations 1981 were originally provided for under Regulation 5, which suggested that all the rights, powers, duties and liabilities under the contract of employment passed post-transfer (although pension rights were excluded from this general principle, as is discussed in greater detail in Chapter 3). Regulation 5(5) gave rise to the right of any employee to terminate the contract of employment without notice if there was a substantial and detrimental change to the working conditions. Regulation 6 provided for the post-transfer continuation of existing collective agreements made with recognised trade unions on behalf of employees whose contracts of employment were preserved by Regulation 5(1).

Fundamental to the 1981 TUPE framework was Regulation 8 which provided protection from dismissal either pre- or post-transfer. In the event of dismissal, then the affected employees were (and are) granted protection under Part X and s. 218 of the ERA 1996 for unfair dismissal, with the business transfer as the reason or principal reason for their dismissal. Such dismissals will be automatically deemed unfair, unless the reason for the

---

[11] Berriman v. Delabole Slate Ltd [1985] ICR 546 CA

dismissal is based on an ETO ground, and can be supported by changes brought about either by the transferee or transferor, either pre- or post-transfer. To date, these defences have not generated many cases in the UK.

Trade union recognition was affirmed in Regulation 9, conditional upon the fact that there is a 'relevant transfer'. The duty to inform and consult recognised trades unions in *"long enough time before a relevant transfer to enable consultations to take place"* was provided for in accordance with the ARD guidance. Such consultation or information had to confirm in writing and by post that the transfer was to take place and when, the reasons for it, the legal, economic and social implications of the business transfer, and the measures envisaged in connection with the business transfer. Furthermore, employees were given the right to consult their trades unions and their unions were required to consider affected employees' representations, the whole practice being undertaken on the premise that such be 'reasonably practicable'.

Consequently, should the transferor have failed to inform or consult, then the trade union concerned could have presented a complaint to an Employment Tribunal. The ECJ's ruling in *Wren & Others v Eastbourne Borough Council & UK Western Control Ltd*[12] reiterated that Regulation 10 invoked the question of the 'reasonably practicable' circumstances of the situation in which the employer was expected to perform such tasks as consultation and 'seeking agreement' with the workforce on the business transfer. If the ET deemed the employer to be in breach of those duties imposed in Regulation 10, an order under Regulation 11(11) for a compensatory award of two weeks' pay (later amended in 1993 to four weeks' pay and then in 1999 to 13 weeks' pay) could be made. Regulations 8, 10 and 11 were inapplicable to those employed abroad (i.e. outside the UK or ordinarily an employee on board a ship outside the UK, despite that ship being registered in the UK). Regulation 14 allowed for any consequential amendments to the Regulations, as belatedly and eventually occurred in 2006.

These controversial 1981 Regulations fuelled much of the litigation and debate about the effectiveness of the laws on business transfers. Many of these cases have seriously questioned whether the 1981 TUPE Regulations 1981 did, in fact, adequately implement the 1977 ARD. The case law from 1986 to 2006, evidences that this objective was subverted by arguments

---

[12] Wren & others v. Eastbourne Borough Council & UK Waste Control Ltd [1993] IRLR 425/[1993] ICR 955 EAT and [1993] 3 CMLR 166 ECJ

framed centrally around the 1981 Regulations, in order to evade the duties imposed by the Directive. Furthermore, the weak provisions central to protecting employees, consultation and information, demonstrated how ineffective the 1981 TUPE regulatory framework was becoming in practice.

2.4. ECJ's Case Law: 1985-2006

Between 1985 and 2006, the ECJ ruled 32 times on the ARD, the principal purpose of these ECJ rulings being to assist EU Member States with their interpretation of the obligations arising under the 1977 ARD. An important ruling from the ECJ was that of *Schmidt*[13], where the ECJ ruled that the contracting-out of a single cleaner came within the scope of the ARD and so could constitute a relevant transfer. In particular, the ECJ stressed that the absence of tangible assets and the fact that the employment is an ancillary activity and performed by a single employee are not decisive factors for the purpose of establishing a transfer. The significance of *Schmidt* was the ECJ's conclusion that the retention of its identity is the decisive criterion for establishing whether a business transfer has occurred. In support of this was Advocate-General Van Gerven's question as to: *"...whether the cessation of a specific operation within an undertaking and the consequent transfer of that operation to an outside undertaking is to be regarded as a transfer of a part of the undertaking within the meaning of the Directive?"*.

An answer to this question was given by the ECJ in *Schmidt*, in holding that contracting-out is clearly within the scope of the ARD. Previously in *Rask*, a case concerning the tendering out of the operational running of a canteen service, ECJ had reaffirmed the 'retention of identity' test and categorically included contracting-out within the scope of the ARD. The ECJ's growing jurisprudence has been immensely helpful in clarifying the ARD. In particular, the ECJ's ruling in:

Spijkers, which established the criteria for identifying 'a legal transfer', played a significant role in the development of the law relating to business transfers;

Redmond, including public and private undertakings under the ambit of the ARD;

Rask, including business transfers brought about by contracting out within the scope of the ARD; and

Katsikas[14], granting employees a right to resign should they disagree with the business transfer,

---

[13] Schmidt v. Spar-und Leikhasse der fruheren Amter Bordesholm [1994] IRLR 302 ECJ

[14] Katsikas v. Konstantinidis [1988] 2 CMLR 265 ECJ 15

highlight the growing important influence of EC law in this area.

As already discussed, the *Schmidt* judgment met with strong criticism from many EU governments. In particular, some German lawyers refused to accept that an activity can be transferred without a transfer of goodwill and business knowledge. This ECJ ruling strongly influenced the UK courts in the *Dines*[15] case. Fuelling the controversy surrounding the scope of the ARD, the ECJ's ruling in the *Rygaard*[16] case, concerning a firm of carpenters who were contracted to construct a canteen, contains some of the German disapproval of the *Schmidt* ruling. In *Rygaard*, following the bankruptcy of the main contractor, the carpenters, who had been made redundant as a consequence, were transferred to the sub-contractor to complete the work. Ole Rygaard, one of the carpenters affected, sought damages for wrongful dismissal. Considering all the facts and applying the ECJ's previous ruling in *Spijkers*, the ECJ, disagreeing with the Advocate-General, held that there was no transfer where one undertaking merely made available to another certain workers and materials for carrying out particular works. The ECJ reasoned that the making available of workers and materials did not of itself constitute a stable economic activity as no assets had been transferred. Thus, such a failure meant that certain activities formerly undertaken by the transferor could not be transferred. This ruling suggests that the ECJ might be retreating from its earlier position in the *Schmidt* ruling.

The ECJ's ruling in *Merckx*[17], concerning the transferring of a one area dealership to another dealer, restated the Court's reasoning in *Schmidt* that one person is sufficient for a transfer, as is one entity. In *Merckx*, two salesmen sued Ford when it discontinued its dealership held by their employer Anfo Motors, having passed it over to another independent dealer, Novarobel. Novarobel took on only 14 of Anfo's 64 existing employees. The business transfer also incurred a change in location. In the ECJ's view, no contractual relationship between the parties was necessary for a business transfer. Thus, following this reasoning the ECJ held that any replacement of an outgoing contractor by a successful, incoming contractor is a relevant business transfer and one which is covered by the ARD despite there being no passing of tangible assets. In this case the ECJ ruled that the employees had a right to object to the business transfer and claim

---

15 Dines v. Initial Health Care Services and Pall Mall Services Group Ltd [1993] ICR 978 EAT and [1994] IRLR 336 CA

16 Rygaard Ledernes Hovedorganisation v. Dansk [1995] IRLR 51 ECJ

17 Merckx v. Ford Motors Co. [1996] IRLR 467 ECJ 18

compensation in circumstances where they were being compelled to change employer and take up employment on worse terms and conditions.

In *Henke*[18], a case concerning the reorganisation of municipal administration, the ECJ held that legal secretaries and other administrative staff working for local authorities in Germany could be dismissed or have their terms and conditions changed as a consequence of a business transfer between a former local authority and a contractor. In this terse ruling by the ECJ, Mrs Henke's dismissal as a mayor's secretary when the municipal administration was transferred to the regional authority could now open the floodgates and allow many contracting-out exercises involving administrative staff to avoid the ARD. The ECJ's reasoning was based on the failure of these administrative workers to constitute a stable economic entity, as service providers, capable of being the subject of a business transfer. Such a ruling has wide-ranging implications for many contracting-out scenarios, unless the decision in *Henke* is narrowly read to be applicable only to those activities which are administrative and not wholly economic in nature.

Similarly, the ECJ in *Suzen*[19] argued that a cleaning contract to clean a church-run secondary school in Bonn which was terminated with one contractor and awarded to another, giving rise to eight dismissals on the grounds of redundancy, did not by the mere fact that the services provided by the old and new contractors were similar support the conclusion that a business transfer had taken place. In his Opinion Advocate-General La Pergola went further and contended that the transfer of a bare service contract from an outgoing to an incoming contractor, where no tangible or intangible assets were passing, did not constitute a business transfer within the scope of the ARD. The ECJ held in *Suzen* that a single transfer of activities was of itself insufficient to amount to a transfer of an undertaking. Rejecting the Advocate-General's opinion, the ECJ reaffirmed the orthodox 'economic entity' test which had been developed in *Spijkers* and later refined in *Schmidt* and *Merckx*. Thus, no relationship need exist between the transferor and transferee prior to the transfer for the ARD to apply, but the passing of tangible assets or the taking-over of a workforce remain as pre-requisites for meeting the *Spijkers* test. Had the ECJ followed the Advocate-General's advice, the *Suzen* decision would have impacted on all contracted labour-only services. What is interesting from a British

---

[18] Henke v. Gereinde Schierke [1996] IRLR 701 ECJ

[19] Suzen v. Zehnacker Gebaudereinigung GmbH Krankenhausservice [1997] IRLR 255 ECJ

perspective is that the *Suzen* case directly conflicts with the EAT's approach adopted in *Birch v. Nuneaton & Bedworth Borough Council*, where the transfer of the Council's leisure facilities to an external contractor, who was responsible for actually providing similar activities, albeit in different hands, was held to be sufficient to amount to a business transfer as the identity of the undertaking is retained. Such conflict leaves the UK courts in a quandary, although the Court of Appeal (upholding the supremacy of EC law) upheld the *Suzen* ruling in its decision in the *Betts* case, discussed below in detail. However, it remains a salient fact that despite this recent legal conservatism on the part of the ECJ, had the ECJ adhered to the Advocate-General's Opinion in *Suzen*, the court's narrowing of the scope of the ARD would have been advanced more radically than at present. In any event, it can be contended that the *Schmidt* ruling remains the high-water mark on the ARD's application, since except for *Henke*, *Suzen* and *Rygaard*, which it could be argued are rulings confined to their facts, the ECJ's jurisprudence since 1985 has been one which has emphasised their concern about defending the ARD's primary purpose: to protect employees subject to business transfers.

The ECJ's rulings, in *Hildago*[20] and *Collino*[21], however, did very little, except to remind all concerned with business transfers that employees subjected to a business transfer are transferred automatically by the mere fact of the transfer and thus, from that moment onwards the employee is legally employed by the transferee. It thus follows from this sacrosanct principle of automatic transfer, that contracts of employment transfer as a matter of law, irrespective of whether the employer or employee knows that a business transfer has occurred.

More confusion was created in 2001, when the ECJ in *Oy Liikenne Ab v. Liskojarvi & Juntunen*[22], a transfer involving the contracting-out of Finnish buses, concluded that because no buses had been transferred no transfer could have occurred. Despite transferring 33 of the 45 employees, none of the 26 buses nor other assets were transferred and the ECJ as a result ruled that whilst labour-intensive operations might be subjected to a transfer, other factors had to be considered where the relevant undertaking depended on the use of substantial assets. To that end, the ECJ took the

---

[20] Sanchez Hildago v. Associacion de Servicios ASEH and Sociedad Cooperativa Minerva [1999] IRLR 136 ECJ

[21] Collino and Chiappero v. Telecom Italia [2000] IRLR 788 ECJ

[22] Oy Likenne Ab v. Liskojarvi and Juntunnen [2001], C-172/99, 25 January 2001, ECJ

view that a bus service operation needed buses and therefore the provision of such a service could not be viewed as a service based on labour alone. In this case, a contracting-out transfer was excluded from the Directive/TUPE's remit.

Three years later, the ECJ in *Abler v. Sodexho*[23] held that there was a transfer that fell within the meaning of business transfer found in Article 1 of the 1977 Directive since in an equipment-based sector such as catering, expressly refusing to maintain the employees of a predecessor did not preclude the finding of a business. However, in 2005, in *Celtec Ltd v Astley*[24], the ECJ decided that a date of transfer for the purposes of the 1977 ARD is a particular point in time when responsibility as employer for carrying on the business of the unit transferred moves from the transferor to the transferee. The ECJ came to the conclusion that the date of transfer was therefore *"the date on which responsibility as employer for carrying on the business of the unit transferred moves from the transferor to the transferee"*. The Court went on to note that it was well established that that date could not be postponed by the will of the transferor or the transferee. It should be noted that the ruling of the ECJ contradicts the opinion of the Advocate-General, who had thought it possible to abandon the attempt to pinpoint a particular date as being the 'date of transfer' in these circumstances, provided certain conditions were met.

2.4.1. Postscript

Even with the TUPE Regulations 2006 now truly established, the former Directive 77/187 continues to wreak havoc with the Supreme Court's referral of *Parkwood Leisure Ltd v. Alemo-Herron*[25]. The issue before the ECJ is whether Article 3(1) of the 1977 Directive precludes national courts from giving a dynamic interpretation to the TUPE Regulations 1981. Further, the ECJ in C-426/11 *Alemo-Herron v. Parkwood* responded in the affirmative and that such a preclusion is justifiable given the inherent balance to be struck between employee and employer interests. The ECJ's ruling reaffirms the principle of freedom of contract in TUPE dealings which underpins a majority, if not all, TUPE transactions.

---

[23] Abler v. Sodexho [2004] IRLR 168, ECJ

[24] Celtec v. Astley [2005] (Case C-478/03), 26 May 2005, ECJ

[25] Parkwood Leisure Ltd v. Alemo-Herron [2011] UKSC

2.5.   UK judicial guidance, 1987-2006

The caseload of business transfers litigation has been ever increasing since 1989, somewhat like Lord Denning's infamous 'incoming tide'. Not only has the common law developed at EU level, but at domestic level the pace of litigation has also been rapid. This is reflected in Scott Baker J.'s statement in the *Betts*[26] case at first instance: *"I cannot believe that the legal position is so finely tuned that laymen cannot normally tell from the outset whether TUPE applies"*. In response to that statement, it is the legal confusion surrounding TUPE which has caused much of the litigation.

The UK courts' most important TUPE ruling on business transfers was that delivered by the House of Lord's ruling in *Litster*. Since 1989, *Litster* has provided a timely reminder that the ARD seeks to safeguard employees' rights, when subjected to business transfers. Their Lordships held in *Litster* that the: *"UK courts are under a duty to give a purposive construction to Directives and to Regulations issued for the purpose of complying with Directives"*. As in the *Dines* case, the *Litster* decision clearly exposes a fundamental clash of philosophies between domestic and Community laws, particularly in respect of contracting-out. The Court of Appeal in *Dines*, provides authoritative confirmation that the contracting-out of services, including a change of contractor as a result of a CCT exercise, will usually be covered by TUPE.

Dines is a landmark case in the context of the UK's development of its judicial reasoning on the purpose of TUPE. Mrs Dines, and others, initiated proceedings in the ET on the grounds of unfair dismissal by reason that both her old and new employers had failed to give effect to the TUPE Regulations 1981. The ET concluded that since the new employer had introduced their own management, equipment, stock or supplies and because there was no transfer of goodwill between the cleaning contractors, then no business transfer had occurred. The following extract of the ET's decision was to take on a crucial significance when the case came before the Court of Appeal:

"The fact that the business is not sold does not mean that there cannot be a transfer within the meaning of the Regulations. However when one company enters into competition with a number of other companies to obtain a contract as happened in this case and a different company wins the contract from the company that was previously providing the services then this is a cessation of the business of the first contractors on the hospital premises, and the commencement of a new business by

---

[26] Betts v. Brintel Helicopters Ltd; [1996] IRLR 45 HC and [1997] IRLR 361 CA

[Pall Mall] when they are awarded the contract. The fact that [Pall Mall] employed the same workforce at the same workplace is not in this case a factor giving rise to a transfer under the Regulations for the reasons given in this decision".

The ET had decided that there had not been a complete transfer of staff and, in any event, transfer of personnel was only one factor to be taken into account. The ET concluded there had been no transfer of equipment, goodwill, or other tangible assets; nor of any distinctive way of working. Subsequently, upon appeal, the EAT rejected the suggestion that the ET had misdirected itself in any way or that its decision was perverse.

In the Court of Appeal, it was maintained that the question as to whether there had been a business transfer or not admitted of only an affirmative answer. Applying the criteria established in *Spijkers*, already discussed, the services consisted of the provision of labour only; the labour force remained the same; the nature of the scope of the services provided were identical; the place at which the services undertaken were the same; and the services were provided for the same customer, namely Basildon and Thurrock Health Authority. Eventually, it was accepted in the *Dines* case that the cleaning services at the Orsett Hospital were an undertaking.

In contrast to *Dines*, is the Court of Appeal's approach in *Betts*, a case concerning the contracting-out of helicopter services and the redeployment of existing staff to the 'new' contractor. Their Lordships held that where the labour force was not the only asset of the operation and a vast majority of its assets were retained, it could not be said that the undertaking was transferred. In the words of Kennedy LJ: *"With the benefit of Suzen we are satisfied that the proper approach was to consider first the nature of... the operation.... As to this issue... there was no transfer of the undertaking so that it retained its identity".* Thus, in deciding whether an operation was an undertaking for the purposes of TUPE, the court had to look beyond the activity entrusted to it. Since in most cases there would be land, buildings, plant and staff all contributing to the undertaking, whilst these would be sufficient to sustain an undertaking and an economic activity, such would be insufficient for the purposes of determining whether a transfer of an undertaking has taken place. Such a juxtaposition by the Court of Appeal towards its judgment in *Dines*, now causes only to confuse the law further, making it harder for all concerned with business transfers within the UK to determine whether TUPE applies or not. It appears that the progress previously made could now have been temporarily obscured. However, since the Court of Appeal relied upon the ECJ's ruling in *Schmidt* in *Dines*, it emerges that the only bewilderment with the ARD in the courts consists of whether to apply *Schmidt* or *Suzen* in deciding whether an undertaking is transferable for the purposes of TUPE in each individual case.

On the theme of a part transfer of a business the EAT in *Buchanan-Smith v. Schleicher & Co. International Ltd*[27] considered the issue of the transfer of employees who were not solely working in the entity transferred. Mrs Buchanan-Smith was a director of a company which sold spare parts and serviced equipment. However, the sales division was closed down and the servicing and parts departments were transferred to Schleicher. In the course of submissions to the EAT, Schleicher maintained that this transfer was only a sale of assets. This argument was rejected by the EAT and it was held that a business transfer could be established on the basis that the identity had been retained.

In the significant case of *Wilson v. St Helens Borough Council*[28] 'old' wounds regarding the usage of compromise agreements were reopened. The facts of the case were that Wilson was one of a number of employees, employed in a Council controlled care home which had been transferred from Lancashire County Council to St Helens Borough Council. The transfer of the home constituted was a business transfer accompanied by a change in terms and conditions. There was no evidence that the new terms had been accepted by the employees. The ET found that employees should not and did not sign away their rights and the EAT held that employers could buy out rights of employees, as they could dismiss and re-engage employees on new terms, and that no detrimental change to them could occur, as TUPE preserved employee's rights. As Mummery J. succinctly put it:

"It is true that there may be cases where an effective variation of the terms of employment does take place subsequently either by express agreement or by agreement inferred from conduct...[but] the law, surprising though it may be to English legal tradition, is clear. If the operative reason for the variation is the transfer of the undertaking, then the variation will be invalid".

However, on appeal, in the joined cases of *Wilson and Meade*[29], the Court of Appeal held that the existence of a business transfer itself did not justify a dismissal, unless the dismissal was for economic, organisational or technical reasons, as prescribed for in Regulation 8 of the TUPE Regulations 1981. For Wilson, this meant that for an ET to find a variation

---

[27] Buchanan-Smith v. Schleicher & Co. Intl Ltd; [1996] IRLR 547 EAT

[28] Wilson v. St Helens BC [1996] IRLR 320 EAT & [1996] IRLR 505 CA

[29] Meade v. British Fuels Ltd [1996] IRLR 541 EAT

in terms and conditions justifiable after a business transfer, ETO reasons would have to be found, and not solely that a transfer had taken place. Without these ETO reasons, any variation to terms and conditions became ineffective. In *Meade*, the outcome of the appeal means that an agreement to employment by a former employee of the transferor with the transferee on 'new' terms and conditions were ineffective, albeit that an unfair dismissal claim could be founded. Thus, the EAT had wrongly concluded that a dismissal notice was sufficient to terminate a contract. Clearly, these cases show that applying the *Daddy's Dance Hall*[30] ruling, where it was held that: *"An employee cannot waive the rights conferred upon him by the mandatory provisions of the Acquired Rights Directive 77/187 even if the disadvantages resulting from his waiver are offset from such benefits that, taking the matter as a whole, he is not placed in a worse position"*, can be overturned in some circumstances, but not in others. So, where does the law now stand on the variation of terms and conditions, after a business transfer? That is surely an important question to be addressed in due course by the House of Lords. Hopefully, at last some clarification on the ETO reasons might be given. In the context of these various cases, it appears that the law now makes three salient points:

- in terms of identifying a business transfer, there is now a difference between first and second generation contracting-out;
- a distinction can now be made (despite Kennedy LJ's obiter in *Betts* to the effect that *Suzen* had created *"a shift in emphasis"*), if the facts suggest that it is justifiable, to distinguish between labour intensive and other business transfers; and
- clarity has now been destroyed and legal confusion abounds once more for contractors and employees subjected to business transfers alike.

In 2000 in the case of *Cheesman v. Brewer*[31], the EAT held that the ET had failed to take account of the existing case law. More significantly, it failed to look at things 'in the round', and had failed to consider whether the undertaking had retained its identity. This case highlights how ETs must take account of the ECJ's rulings and that they should apply commonsense to proceedings, whilst applying the relevant legal tests. In both the *ADI (UK) Ltd v. Willer*[32] and *Whitewater Leisure Management Ltd v. Barnes*[33] cases,

---

[30] Foreningen af Arbejdsledere i Danmark v. Daddy's Dance Hall A/S [1988] IRLR 315 ECJ

[31] Cheesman v. Brewer [2000] Unreported, EAT, November 2000

[32] ADI (UK) Ltd v. Willer [2000] EAT, IDS Brief 662 33

[33] Whitewater Leisure Management Ltd v. Burnes [2000] IRLR 456 EAT

where the contracting-out of services has occurred, in applying the *Suzen* ruling the EAT held that as no material assets transferred and a majority of the workforce did not transfer that there could not be a business transfer. Clearly such cases clarify the headache left by *Suzen*, in that following these decisions, labour-intensive transfers are not covered by TUPE. Consequently, the fact that no material assets can be shown to have been transferred results in no transfer of undertaking and therefore TUPE cannot apply.

In *ECM (Vehicle Delivery Services) Ltd v. Cox*[34], multiple transfers took place and the final transferee refused to take on the original transferred staff in order to avoid the application of TUPE. The ET held that TUPE still applied and this was subsequently confirmed by the Court of Appeal. Since *ECM*, the EAT held in the case of *OCS Cleaning (Scotland) Ltd v. Rudden and Olscot Ltd*[35] that TUPE applied even where there were no transfer of assets or none of the existing staff taken on, the reason being the presence of work which was substantially the same after as before the transfer (same customer, same place). Whilst these factors are not conclusive themselves, the message sent out from this decision was that contractors must be aware of a real risk that on any outsourcing or changeover of contractors, TUPE could apply. This approach was confirmed in *RCO Support Services v. UNISON*[36], where the EAT held that *"ancillary services are often staffed with workers with only relatively simple and commonly available skills which on that account TUPE could apply."*

A dismissal is automatically unfair only if it is connected to the business transfer (Regulation 8(1) of the TUPE Regulations 1981). It should be noted that liability for such dismissals passes from the transferor to the transferee. It was originally considered that time was the crucial factor, but this was later deemed not so as was observed in *Taylor v. Connex South Eastern Ltd*[37], where the EAT held that even though four years had elapsed since the transfer, the reason for the dismissal two years after the transfer related to the business transfers. This case reminds us that the key relates to the terms 'connected to' rather than time.

---

[34] ECM (Vehicle Delivery Service) Ltd v. Cox [1998] IRLR 416 CA 35

[35] OCS Cleaning (Scotland) Ltd v. Rudden and Olscot Ltd [1999] Unreported, 29 June 1999, EAT

[36] RCO Support Services v. UNISON [2000] IRLR 624 EAT 37

[37] Taylor v Connex South Eastern Limited, EAT 1243/99, unreported

In a set of peculiar facts in *Euro-Die UK Ltd v. Skidmore*[38], Skidmore's employment ceased with a company who transferred him to Euro-Die. Before being transferred, Skidmore sought a reassurance that his continuity of employment would be preserved. No reassurance was given. Therefore, Skidmore found work elsewhere and claimed constructive dismissal. The EAT upheld the constructive dismissal claim against Euro-Die, the transferee, on the basis that the failure to give a reassurance amounted to a breach of an implied term of trust and confidence.

Clearly the 1977 ARD and the TUPE Regulations 1981 have been supported in part by the ECJ's rulings and clarified or undermined by some of the decisions delivered by the UK's EAT and Court of Appeal. This growing UK common law on TUPE following ECJ rulings should allow both transferor and transferee alike to know whether there is going to be a business transfer without having to await the outcome of litigation. Clearly, Scott Baker J.'s appeal for clarity in the *Betts* case at first instance, has not been answered. In fact, the Court of Appeal, by applying *Suzen* in *Betts*, has added to legal confusion surrounding TUPE and the ARD. Moreover, the legal conflict between the outcomes delivered by the Court of Appeal in both *Dines* and *Betts* has now made it imperative that the House of Lords, which has not ruled on the ARD since *Litster* in 1989, be asked in some later case to resolve this conflict. Alternatively, what is clear from all this case law is that the legal framework governing business transfers was in a state of flux between 1986 and 2006 and was in need of reform.

2.6. Consultation rights conundrum of 1996

The ECJ's 1994 ruling in *Commission v. UK*[39], requiring the UK to implement its obligations under the ARD and Collective Redundancies Directive 75/129 into national law, raised important questions about information, consultation and representation in relation to business transfers. In response to this ruling, the UK government announced its proposals on workers' representatives. This revision arises from Terry Wren's action against Eastbourne Borough Council. Wren and other refuse collectors and street cleaners were given redundancy payments following a contracting-out exercise in the cleaning section of the Borough Council under the Local Government Act 1988. The EAT upheld Wren's and others' appeals and remitted it to another ET for reconsideration. The major issue of concern to Wren and others was their lack of information and Eastbourne Borough

---

[38] EURO-Die UK Ltd v. Skidmore (2000) IDS Brief 655 EAT

[39] Commission v. UK [1994] IRLR 392 and 412 ECJ

Council's failure to consult them. The issue of the provision of information and consultation to workers subjected to business transfers could become further confused with the advent of European Works Councils (EWCs) across the EU under Council Directive 94/45/EC and the Information and Consultation Directive 2001/23/EC, establishing national works councils. Both these Directives provide for the establishment of worker representation in decision-making processes affecting the employer, as well as rights to consultation, information and representation.

2.7. Key TUPE Provisions on Collective rights

TUPE contains provisions which facilitate for constructive relations between employers (both transferor and transferee) and trade unions/elected representatives. The effect of both Regulations 6, 9 and 10 of the TUPE Regulations 1981 was to preserve the existing collective bargaining arrangements on sale of the business. Specifically:

Regulation 6 required that any collective agreement made between the transferor and a trade union shall have effect as if it had been made with the transferee.

Regulation 9 provided that any trade union which was recognised by the transferor shall be deemed to be recognised by the transferee.

Regulation 10 obliged the transferor and transferee to consult with recognised trade unions or elected representatives (in the absence of a recognised trade union) for the purposes of collective consultation under TUPE.

Following the enactment of the Employment Relations Act 1999 (EReLA), as amended 2004, and its institution of legal procedures for the recognition of trades unions within the workplace where there are sufficient members of the workforce who are trade union members, as well as de-recognition procedures, then Regulation 9 became more complex and had to respond to the pace of change brought about by this new legal framework. However, public sector agreements on trade union recognition are more common than private sector arrangements. Consequently, under the TUPE Regulations 1981 the transferee was normally bound by the existing collective agreements and recognition arrangements, but under EReLA the transferee may be able to terminate or modify the arrangements inherited. For instance, the transferee may seek de-recognition. However, the transferee might have had difficulties changing those terms of collective agreements which have already been incorporated into individual employees' contracts, as these once incorporated will become binding. As a result any subsequent changes to collective agreements have to be agreed at a collective level. Alternatively, the transferee can alter a collective agreement which is not legally binding unless it contains a clause indicating that it has legal effect.

As noted above, Regulation 10 of the TUPE Regulations 1981 imposed an obligation to consult collectively before a business transfer occurred. Under Regulation 10, the transferor was initially required to inform and consult with any recognised trade unions in respect of affected employees; i.e. employees subject to the transfer or by measures taken in connection with the transfer. In 1995 (and again, in 1999), the TUPE Regulations 1981 were amended in order to widen the consultation/provision of information obligations so that the obligation became one to consult/inform *"appropriate representatives"*. Appropriate representatives could be either representatives of recognised trade unions (where employees were represented by such a trade union) or in any other cases, employee representatives elected by the employees either for general purposes or specifically in light of the proposed transfer.

The central concern of the *Commission v. UK* ruling was the obligation in the ARD to consult employees recognised as employee representatives, this being an obligation of which the UK was found in breach of. The UK government was required to provide some means or mechanism by which non-employee representatives will be consulted. The TUC desired a Code of Practice, whereas the UK government's response was to establish penalties under the revised TUPE Regulations 2006, discussed in Chapter 6. This ruling placed much more emphasis on the issue of representation in terms of consultation being the key to safeguarding rights under business transfers. This ECJ ruling, however, poses mixed blessings, since it addresses the issue of consultation which can be achieved by mixed systems of elected representatives or representative unions.

The fundamental problem was the definitional ambiguity which surrounds the term 'representativeness' in a workplace context. What does it mean in the employment environment? The response to that question is determined by answering two further questions, whether trade unions should have participation rights in a workplace dialogue and where it is accepted that trade unions have these rights, what forms of dialogue, or mechanisms, are in place? This reasoning also encounters a further difficulty, insofar as we must define what a 'trade union' is. This is problematical because there are three options to explore before answering the question. Essentially, should one take the statutory definition found in s.1 of the TULRCA 1992; or does 'trade union' status depends upon registration as a union, or alternatively, does it depend upon certification or recognition under the EReLA? Given English law's current stance, management often determine what is meant by 'representativeness', which is usually dependent upon which union is recognised, if any, for bargaining purposes.

As a concept, 'representativeness' is important for collective bargaining reasons. Information channels are indeed vital to those workers subjected to transfers. Despite these ideals for 'representativeness' and its consultation and bargaining functions, the trend today in the UK is towards de-recognition and falling unionisation rates. In contrast, the EU is creating social partnership and promoting social dialogue. In a British context, the TUC has recently reclaimed statutory recognition rights. As representativeness is directly linked to membership levels and currently where trade union density is less than 30% and less than 50% of the workforce are covered by collective bargaining, UK employers are either more willing, or have no other choice but, to hold workplace elections. This is not unique to the UK. In France, plant level elections take place, as a means of determining what and who is 'representative' for bargaining purposes. These problems might explain the reasons behind the UK's reluctance to accept the ECJ's ruling and the consultation obligations provided for in the ARD and TUPE. The UNISON case, involving the business transfer of an hospital to NHS Trust status, showed that even if an employer does not fulfil the requisite consultation regulations, then the sanction of four weeks' pay, (now thirteen weeks pay) compensation does very little as a deterrent.

2.8. The Collective Redundancies and Transfer of Undertakings (Protection of Employment) (Amendment) Regulations 1999

These Regulations, commonly referred to as the 1999 Consultation Regulations, came into force on 28 July 1999 and apply (in respect of TUPE transfers) to transfers that completed after 1 November 1999. They ended much of the uncertainty presented in the provisions of earlier analogous Regulations dating from 1995 and require the information and consultation to be take place with trade union representatives, if the employees affected are represented by a recognised trade union. Where no such trade union exists or applies, the transferor can choose whether to inform/consult with employee representatives who have been elected and hold the authority to receive information and be consulted on behalf of affected employees, or to hold elections for ad hoc representatives for the purposes of the TUPE transfers. As a result these Regulations establish two key stages for information and consultation:

Stage 1

Prior to the consultation, where no recognised trade union applies, the transferor and transferee should take the following steps:

- consider the number of representatives required;
- correspond with all employees affected (including those absent, on sick leave) and request nominations;
- correspond with nominees and confirm 'willingness';
- explain role of elected representatives to nominees;
- distribute secret ballot forms to all employees affected; and
- count the ballot and notify representatives.

Stage 2

Having elected the representatives, the transferor/transferee should take the following steps:

- meet with the representatives;
- ensure that the elected representatives meet with other employees to establish views;
- consider representatives views; and
- confirm outcomes to all employees It should be noted that where an employer does all the above steps, but fails to obtain elected representatives for whatever reasons, but a genuine opportunity to elect such representatives has occurred, then the employer has discharged his duty/obligations under TUPE. Proof of such, though, will be required should this be challenged in the future. Therefore, keeping records of meetings, and employee communications and similar matters is essential. The key here is to establish a reasonable time schedule.

Regulation 10(3) of the TUPE Regulations 1981 required the transferee to notify the transferor of any measures envisaged taking effect after the transfer, so as to enable this information to be given to the affected employees. The transferee was, however, not obliged to consult prior to the transfer with those affected by the transfer.

It is important to understand that these changes under the 1999 Consultation Regulations influenced the drafting of the TUPE Regulations 2006 (to be discussed in Chapter 6). In particular, they led to the realisation that the transferor should consider the following practical implications in order to ensure 'proper' informing and consulting is taking place:

- whether the agreed arrangements for information/consultation cover all the employees affected;

- whether sufficient time has been given at all stages (nominations, elections, meetings);
- whether the employees can 'freely vote' (i.e. no intimidation, etc);
- the need to confirm total number of employees who must be represented and the various locations, subdivisions;
- the need to clarify the terms of office of the representatives;
- the need to confirm 'confidentiality' rules with regard to consultation/information with the elected representatives; and
- the practical necessity of utilising the services of an independent scrutineer to count ballot(s). One problem may remain, even under the 2006 TUPE regime, for certain types of transfer, namely that those that are commercially sensitive. To seek to elect ad hoc representatives for a 'sensitive transfer' may be difficult. Consequently, two options prevail:
  1. to convert an existing body into a body of representatives for consultation (e.g. another permanent body, such as an EWC or a Health and Safety Committee); or
  2. to consult with individual employees on a direct basis. See the *Humphreys v. University of Oxford*[40] case for an example. This situation of secrecy will be particularly true where the Stock Exchange Rules on Mergers and Take-Overs applies.

In such circumstances the non-compliance with TUPE may be justified where a breach of other regulatory rules would occur (see Regulation 15(2) of the TUPE Regulations 2006 – Special Circumstances Defence). These exceptions, however, are likely to be narrowly construed by the courts/tribunals. The Court of Appeal in *Humphreys v. University of Oxford*, considered a situation where before a transfer an employee is made aware of the fact that there will be substantial and/or detrimental changes to the contract of employment or working conditions. The Court held that the employee could object to the transfer and resign (claiming constructive dismissal against the transferee).

Above all, the 1999 Consultation Regulations required the transferor to ensure that 'the elections are fair and that sufficient representatives to represent the interests of all affected employees are in place and that the requisite information and consultation is completed'. This lives on and is reinforced in the TUPE Regulations 2006.

---

[40] Humphreys v. University of Oxford [2000] IRLB 635 CA

TUPE: LAW & PRACTICE

2.9. Practical Issues post-1999 Consultation Regulations

A number of practical issues remain to be addressed under the TUPE Regulations 2006, in respect of the consultation process such as the rights of the elected representatives, timescales, information obligations, consultation rights and remedies.

2.9.1. Elected Representatives

Once elected the employer must provide facilities and assistance. For example, good access must be given to the relevant employees/ workforce(s). Elected representatives also have the right to paid time-off during the working day to execute their duties as a representative or undergoing training. Note also that any dismissals of elected representatives will be treated as automatically unfair if the reason is that the employee was an elected representative under TUPE (or standing as a nominee in a TUPE elected representatives ballot). No such elected representatives should suffer any detriment whilst undertaking their duties or function as an elected representative.

2.9.2. Timescales

It is imperative that throughout the consultation process reasonable time is given. Regulation 10(2) of the TUPE Regulations 1981 provided that information about the transfer must be given to the representatives 'long before the transfer to enable consultation to take place' (analogous provisions are contained in Regulation 13(2) of the TUPE Regulations 2006). Whilst TUPE does not set out clear timescales, transferors should be careful not to rush the process. Unlike redundancy consultation where timescales are set, clearly TUPE implicitly requires 'meaningful dialogue' about the economic, social and legal implications. "Good time" may be 45 days (following the redundancy model) so as to allow for meaningful consultation 'with a view to reaching agreement' on the key issues.

2.9.3. Information obligations

Regulation 10(2) of the TUPE Regulations 1981 ensured that the transferor should provide the elected representatives with information on: the facts of the transfer (date and reasons); the 'legal, social and economic' implications (as perceived by the transferee) for the affected employees; what measures are envisaged, post-transfer; and any other information provided or measures envisaged by the transferee. (Again, analogous provisions survived under the TUPE Regulations 2006, as discussed in Chapter 6). Regulation 10(3) required the transferee to notify the transferor of any information appropriate to be given to the elected representatives. In practice, the precise meaning of the technical terms 'measures' and 'envisaged' can sometimes pose problems. In *IPCS v. Secretary of State for Defence*[41], it was held that the term 'measures' encompassed any action or step envisaged by the employer as affecting the transferred employees. For example, consequential redundancies or alterations to working practices or contracts of employment. Moreover, 'envisaged' was considered to mean a measure formulated from a proposal or coherent plan relating to the business transfer.

2.9.4. Consultation rights

Regulation 10(5) of the TUPE Regulations 1981 required that consultation should be conducted 'with a view to seeking the [elected] representatives' agreement to measures to be taken'.[42] To that end, consultation only commences following information which leads to the transferor/transferee envisaging taking measures in connection with the transfer (i.e. redundancies, changes to contracts, changes to working conditions/practices, union de-recognition or union recognition, or any changes whatsoever).

2.9.5. Remedies

Any breach of Regulation 10 of the TUPE Regulations 1981 could potentially lead to a complaint being brought before an ET under the (then) Regulation 11 on the grounds of failure to comply (i.e. electoral defects; no or lack of information; no, limited or lack of consultation; lack of trade union recognition; or any other case affecting employees). Sanctions continue to be available under the 2006 TUPE regime. These are discussed in greater detail in Chapter 6; however, broadly speaking, where an ET upholds the complaint, a Declaration is given and the transferor will be required to pay 13 weeks' pay (before 1 January 1999 it was 4 weeks under the 1995 Regulations to each employee affected. Note that the week's pay is NOT subject to the maximum limit of £280 per week for these purposes.

2.10. Revising the Directive

Following over 40 rulings from the ECJ on the ARD, the EU Council agreed in 1998 to amend the Directive, after four years of political and legal wrangling amongst the EU institutions and Member States. Subsequently, in March 1996, the House of Lords Select Committee on the European Communities, Sub-Committee 'E' on 'EU Law and Institutions,' published its Report on the EU Commission's proposed revised text. After hearing

---

[41] IPCS v. Secretary of State for Defence [1987] IRLR 373 EAT

[42] See also Regulation 13(6) of the TUPE Regulations 2006.

evidence from academics, representatives from both the unions and business, legal practitioners and others, it emerged that the main areas of controversy related to the scope of the ARD; the inclusions of share transfers, pensions, sea-going vessels and insolvency situations; mandatory introduction of joint liability for a minimum of twelve months after the transfer; and the rights to information and consultation. Other matters which proved to be almost as equally contentious concerned whether or not judicial authorities should be permitted to change terms and conditions and the setting of the threshold for applicability to which the ARD applies at the level of 50 employees. Two major concerns within the Committee were whether to maintain the exclusion of pension provision protection in the ARD and to reinforce the consultation rights, despite ECJ rulings on both these issues.

Professor Sir Bob Hepple QC in his written submission to the UK House of Lord's Committee outlined the general shortcomings of the existing 1977 directive, namely the unclear scope of the directive. In his evidence to the Committee, Professor Hepple suggested that the revised article 1 was *"wrong in principle"* and did not achieve the clarity desired. As Lord Slynn later summarised the position in a debate on the report: *"Representatives of both employers and employees thought that this was not a helpful distinction to introduce between 'activity' and 'economic entity' particularly as it was thought that some activities could themselves constitute an economic entity"* (See Hansard HL 4 June 1996, col. 1192). CBI concerns centred upon the inclusion of contracting-out under the scope of the directive, which the case law had already achieved. In seeking some moderation in this blanket application, the CBI submitted that: *"...the current situation damages contracting-out"*, resulting in delays in tendering and higher administrative costs and distorted competition. They also vehemently opposed the inclusion of pension rights under the Directive. The TUC, whilst welcoming the EU Commission's attempts to clarify the law, were sceptical of its intentions should the proposed revisions seek to distort the ECJ's rulings.

The Law Society advocated that the threshold of employees to which the ARD applied should be lowered to 20, in common with other recently enacted UK legislation, such as the Disability Discrimination Act 1995. The Employment Law Association (ELA) desired more differentiation between an economic entity and activity. They suggested that if the purpose of revised Article 1(1) in the 1998 ARD was to exclude such cases as *Schmidt*, then it had failed to do so. The ELA considered the implications of joint liability unfavourable, particularly in terms of equal pay, and were concerned that the inclusion of share transfers would alter the Directive, as it no longer necessarily protects acquired rights, but could create 'new' ones.

Having heard all of the evidence their Lordships' Committee, consisting of eminent practitioners, experts and academics, made the following main recommendations:

i.   to reject the Commission's proposed amendment to Article 1;
ii. share transfers should be included under the Directive;
iii. non-liquidation proceedings should be included under the Directive;
iv. to reject the Commission's joint liability proposal;
v.   an EU definition of the term 'employee' should be provided for the ARD;
vi. to support the proposed changes bringing the text of Article 6 into line with the equivalent provisions of the Collective Redundancies Directive. But that the 50 employees threshold should be lowered to 20;
vii. agree to extend the scope of the Directive to include sea-going vessels; and
viii.the Commission should consider the inclusion of 'comparable' pension rights.

The Committee also recommended that further clarity was required in respect of Articles 2(2); 4(1); and 4(5). In particular, their Lordships advocated greater clarity on the criteria required to identify a 'stable economic entity'. Following from these comments and the concerns raised by the European Parliament, the EU Council received a final revised version of the Amended ARD in 1998 at the Cardiff Summit.

2.11. Amended Directive – 1998

The 1977 ARD did not prove easy to apply in practice and has proved to be particularly controversial in relation to contracting-out and out-sourcing. It has resulted in significant number of cases being referred from domestic courts to the European Court of Justice for interpretation. The European Commission tendered proposals to amend the 1977 Directive in 1994. A revised draft was published in 1997 following heavy criticism of the initial proposals by the European Parliament. The most significant change to the original draft was the EU Commission's abandonment of its attempt to clarify the definition of transfer of a business or part of a business by seeking to exclude a transfer of only an activity. Other important proposed amendments related to the liability for pre-transfer debts to employees; the inclusion of state pension provisions within the scope of the ARD, whilst retaining the exclusion of other pension provisions; the inclusion of insolvency situations; and the information and consultation provisions.

A minor success of the UK's Presidency of the Council of Ministers during the first six months of 1998 was to secure the agreement to adopt the Directive amending the Acquired Rights Directive at the Cardiff Summit. The Amending Directive inserted new Articles 1-7b into the 1977 Directive and the revisions had to be implemented by EU Member States within three year period from 29 June 1998, the date of adoption. We will now consider the amending provisions in detail, analysing the potential employment relations implications and identifying some missed opportunities in terms of other possible revisions.

Determining the precise scope of application of the 1977 ARD has involved the ECJ being requested to provide interpretative rulings on a relatively frequent basis. The main problem has related to the issue of whether the ARD embraces the contracting-out of services. In an attempt to clarify matters, the EU Commission had originally proposed adding a new second paragraph to Article 1(1) of the Directive, with the aim of excluding from its scope a transfer of a mere activity of an undertaking as opposed to the transfer an economic entity. The proposal met with substantial criticism from all sides and it was eventually withdrawn by the EU Commission.

Unfortunately, the amended formulation which was ultimately adopted, based on words from a number of European cases, without relying exclusively on any of these, also offers us little in the way of clarification or guidance. Article 1(b) states that there is a transfer *"where there is a transfer of an economic entity which retains its identity, meaning an organised grouping of resources which has the objective of pursuing an economic activity, whether or not that activity is central or ancillary"*. Given the brevity of this definition, we are forced to go back to the case law. Indeed, Recital 4 of the Amending Directive specifically emphasizes that the "clarification" offered by the new Article 1:*"does not alter the scope of Directive 77/187/EEC as interpreted by the Court of Justice."* Given that it was the confused state of the case law which prompted demands for a revision to the Directive in the first place, this approach is of little assistance in meeting the EU Commission's professed aim of clarification in the interests of *"legal security and transparency"*(Recital 4).

Recent developments in the case law, as we have seen, have exacerbated the problem. The ECJ has enunciated the test as to whether a stable economic entity has been transferred. In *Schmidt*, a case involving a first generation contracting-out, it was held that there could be a transfer of contracted-out cleaning services, even where the services are performed by a single employee and there is no transfer of tangible assets. This approach should be contrasted with the later ruling in *Suzen*, a case relating to second generation contracting-out, that an activity does not, in itself, constitute a stable economic entity. Consequently, the ECJ stated, the mere fact that a similar activity is carried on before and after the change of contractors does not automatically mean that there is a transfer of undertaking. In the case of a labour-intensive undertaking with no significant assets (e.g. contract cleaning) the *Suzen* approach will mean that there will generally be no transfer unless the new contractor takes on the majority of the old contractor's staff. In this decision, the court made no attempt to reconcile its reasoning with the approach adopted in *Schmidt* and signally failed to have regard to the principle of employment protection which underpins the ARD and opened up a possible evasion strategy for transferees. The decision would appear to leave the contractor with the choice as to whether to be bound by taking on the majority of the existing staff. Where the existing workforce is unskilled and easily replaceable there is no incentive to assume responsibilities for the existing workforce. The workforce is relegated to the status of mere assets. As a result, the weakest members of the labour market – the unskilled – are disenfranchised from the protection of the acquired rights legislation.

More recently, in the *Vidal*[43] and *Hidalgo* cases we can observe a possible softening of the *Suzen* approach, though with no clarity in this regard. The focus in these rulings is on whether 'an economic entity' has been transferred, as opposed to whether 'major part of the workforce' has been taken over, as in *Suzen*. This approach seems to lay emphasis on what the undertaking looked like pre-transfer rather than post-transfer and as a result, reduces the possibility that a transferee can evade domestic provisions by refusing to engage the employees in the undertaking transferred. In respect of the provision of services, the ECJ holds that *"an organised grouping of wage earners who are specifically and permanently assigned to a common task may, in the absence of other factors of production, amount to an economic entity"*.

It is frustrating that these recent rulings do not provide clear guidance. In both decisions, the ECJ adopts word-for-word the tests approved in *Suzen*, an approach cynically characterised by Rubenstein as *"jurisprudence by word processor"*. Both *Gomez* and *Sanchez* slavishly adopt the *Suzen* test: *"In order*

---

[43] Francisco Hernandez Vidal Sa v. Gomez [1999] IRLR 132 ECJ

*to determine/consider whether the conditions for a transfer of an entity are met, it is necessary to consider all the facts characterising the transaction in question, including in particular the type of undertaking or business, whether or not its tangible assets, such as buildings and movable property, are transferred, the value of its intangible assets at the time of the transfer, **whether or not the majority of its employees are taken over by the new employer**, whether or not its customers are transferred on before and after the transfer, and the period, if any, for which those activities were suspended. However, all those circumstances are merely single factors in the overall assessment which must be made and therefore cannot be considered in isolation."*

In a British context, it is suggested that a possible route through this confusion would to adopt the purposive approach adopted by Mr. Justice Morrison in *ECM (Vehicle Delivery Services) Ltd v. Cox*, where the Court concluded that it would not be proper for a transferee to be able to control the extent of its obligations by refusing to comply with them in the first place. As Mr. Justice Morrison stated: *"The issue as to whether employees should have been taken on cannot be determined by asking whether they were taken on."* This approach focuses attention on the motive for refusing to take on the existing workforce, so as to decide whether the motivation was avoidance or for some other reason. Even then, there will be difficult questions of proof in establishing the true motive.

The reasoning in *Suzen* comes very close to the EU Commission's original proposal which sought to distinguish the mere transfer of an activity from the transfer of undertaking. Furthermore, it would appear: *"that the Council has set its seal of approval on what the Court of Justice has done so far in interpreting the scope of the Directive, and has left further consideration of this 'hot potato' in the hands of the court".* The EU Council of Ministers has missed an opportunity to offer a guide through this particular legal maze. One possible and preferable option would have been to adopt the British House of Lords Select Committee on the European Communities recommendation (5th Report, Session 1995-96, paragraph 32) that the Directive should give a non-exhaustive list of matters to be taken into account in determining the applicability of the Directive in a particular case without any presumption that the Directive does not apply if one or more of the factors is not present. All the facts and circumstances of the case should be taken into account.

Further problems may be caused by the Amending Directive's exclusion from the scope of the ARD of, *"an administrative reorganisation of public administrative authorities, or the transfer of administrative functions between public administrative authorities"* (Article 1(1)(c)). This follows the earlier decision of the ECJ in *Henke* that the Directive did not apply in such circumstances. It is hard to see how such an approach gives effect to the Directive's principal purpose of employment protection. It is maintained that a preferable view was that adopted by the Advocate General in *Henke* where he stated that the Directive was applicable, *"whenever employees within the meaning of the national protective provisions are employed in an undertaking or an organisational entity"*. As the British TUC pointed out, the ECJ's approach would have posed particular difficulties in Britain during the recent reorganisation of local government, where it was generally assumed throughout that process that the ARD and the domestic regulations were applicable: *"Had Henke been decided earlier, there would have been no guarantee of protection for the thousands of workers affected by reorganisation who would have lost their continuity of employment and other acquired rights"*.

All of these salient issues were duly considered by the DTI, whilst drafting the revised TUPE Regulations 2006. Yet, these Regulations survived a mere seven years before further changes were required, as discussed in Chapters 5 and 6. In the next chapter we consider worker protection in the important area of pensions.

3.   PENSIONS AND TUPE

The treatment of pension rights under TUPE has, arguably, long been anomalous. As has already been noted, Article 3(3) of the 1977 ARD includes an exception to the central tenet of the ARD: that upon the transfer of an undertaking, or part of an undertaking, the transferor's rights, obligations and liabilities arising under the contracts of employment of the transferring employees pass to the transferee. Specifically Article 3(3) excludes from this general principle *"employees' rights to old-age, invalidity or survivors' benefits under supplementary company or inter-company pension schemes outside the statutory social security schemes in Member States"*. This "pensions exclusion" was reflected in Regulation 7(1) of the TUPE Regulations 1981, and since 6 April 2006 has been set out in Regulation 10(1) of the TUPE Regulations 2006. Regulation 10(1) provides that Regulations 4 and 5 (which describe the effect of relevant transfers on contracts of employment and collective agreements and which are discussed in greater detail in Chapter 6) shall not apply:

(a) to so much of a contract of employment or collective agreement as relates to an occupational pension scheme...; or

(b) to any rights, powers, duties or liabilities under or in connection with any such contract or subsisting by virtue of any such agreement and relating to such a scheme or otherwise arising in connection with that person's employment and relating to such a scheme.

Regulation 10(2) provides that for the purposes of Regulation 10(1) (and Regulation 10(3), discussed further below), *"any provisions of an occupational pension scheme which do not relate to benefits for old age, invalidity or survivors shall be treated as not being part of the scheme."*

3.1.   The Pensions Exclusion

For many years, it was widely accepted that the effect of the pensions exclusion was to absolve transferees from any legal obligation to provide any particular type or level of replacement pension provision for transferring employees (especially in the case of business acquisitions). Having said this, as a matter of practical reality, it was often (but by no means always) accepted that some form of replacement pension provision should be provided for transferring employees, if only for the sake of harmonious industrial relations, but the type of replacement pension provision, and the value of benefits so provided, was generally believed to be at the discretion of the transferee.

An exception to this general proposition was (and is) in relation to personal pension schemes (and latterly, in relation to stakeholder pension schemes – at least those established in the form of personal pension schemes, as is usually the case). Such pension arrangements do not fall within the definition of *"occupational pension schemes"* (as defined under section 1(1) of the Pensions Schemes Act 1993) - and thus contractual obligations in respect of personal pension schemes are held to be capable of passing under TUPE from a transferor to a transferee. In practice, however, this generally means that the transferee is simply obliged to continue to contribute to the transferring employees' personal pension schemes at the same rate as that at which the transferor was making contributions immediately before the date of the TUPE transfer, and this is seldom, if ever, a contentious issue.

Historically, the position was not so clear-cut in relation to pension rights arising under occupational pension schemes. There was considerable union and other opposition to the existence of the TUPE pensions exclusion, and a number of attempts were made over the years to restrict or eradicate it. Perhaps the most famous attempt to challenge the provisions of the exclusion was the case of *Warrener v. Walden Engineering Co Ltd*[1] where the Hull Industrial Tribunal was asked to consider whether following a TUPE transfer, a transferee could refuse to provide replacement pension arrangements for transferring employees, notwithstanding that the transferring employees had enjoyed active membership of the transferor's occupational pension scheme immediately before the making of the TUPE transfer. The tribunal held that although the 1977 ARD *"could not protect rights of membership of a particular pension scheme", the occupational pension scheme in question was not a "supplementary pension scheme"* for the purposes of Article 3(3) (because as a pension scheme that was "contracted-out" of the state pension scheme, it stood in place of, rather than "supplemental" to the state pension scheme) and hence did not fall within the scope of the pensions exclusion under the 1977 ARD.

Moreover, the tribunal accepted an argument by Mr Warrener's advocate that the correct method of construing Article 3(3) was to do so on the basis of a narrow interpretation, and that under such an interpretation, Regulation 7 of the TUPE Regulations 1981 did not comply with the 1977 ARD. The tribunal ruled that as a consequence of its findings, the terms of Mr Warrener's contract of employment entitled him to membership of a

---

[1] Warrener v. Walden Engineering Company Limited [1993] IRLR 179

replacement occupational pension scheme (post-transfer) and that the terms of such membership should be no less favourable than those applying to his previous (pre-transfer) employment.

The transferee appealed the decision of the tribunal, and in June 1993, the EAT overturned the tribunal's ruling (*Walden Engineering Co. Ltd v Warrener*[2]). Specifically, the EAT held that a contracted-out occupational pension scheme is a supplementary scheme for the purposes of the 1977 ARD and the TUPE Regulations 1981, and therefore capable of falling within the exclusion provisions of both pieces of legislation. The EAT also observed that there was no implicit contractual obligation to continue pension arrangements unchanged throughout the currency of the employment relationship. Consequently, there was no legal obligation upon the transferee to provide replacement pension benefits for the transferring employees following the TUPE transfer, notwithstanding that they had enjoyed the provision of such benefits before the date of transfer in respect of pre-transfer service.

The approach adopted by the EAT in the Warrener case was subsequently approved by the High Court in 1996 in the case of *Adams & Others v Lancashire County Council and BET Catering Services Ltd*[3]. In this case, eleven dinner ladies (and several thousand other part-time employees of Lancashire County Council) had their employments transferred from the Council to BET Catering Services Ltd following BET's successful tendering for the Council's school catering service. During their employment with the Council, the dinner ladies (and other employees) had been eligible for membership of, and had accrued benefits under, the Local Government Pension Scheme. Following the transfer of employments to BET, employees earning more than £15,000 per year were offered membership of the BET pension scheme; those transferring employees earning less than £15,000 (including the part-time dinner ladies) were not offered such membership. The dinner ladies brought a test case before the High Court to ascertain whether the refusal of BET to allow them access to BET's pension scheme contravened the 1977 ARD, and whether the TUPE Regulations 1981 properly reflected the provisions of the 1977 ARD.

The High Court, after first observing that these questions had to be considered having regard to the series of decisions in the ECJ which

---

[2] Walden Engineering Co. Ltd. v. Warrener [1993] ICR 967 EAT

[3] Adams v. Lancashire CC & BET Catering Services Ltd [1996] IRLR 154 HC

provide authority that pensions must be regarded as deferred pay[4] held that:

(a) the 1977 ARD makes an exception from its employment protection provisions for all past and future pension rights;

(b) the 1977 ARD requires member states to provide appropriate protection for accrued pension rights; and

(c) the TUPE Regulations 1981 correctly reflect the provisions of the 1977 ARD. The High Court's rulings were subsequently confirmed by the Court of Appeal in 1997; thus it was accepted that an employee's occupational pension rights do not (as a general rule) transfer under TUPE from a transferor to a transferee notwithstanding the transfer of his or her employment.

The issue of the operation of the TUPE pensions exclusion was again revisited by the High Court in 2001 in the case of *Hagen v ICI Chemicals and Polymers Ltd*[5] when the High Court considered a case where the transferor had made various representations to transferring employees about the nature of the transfer exercise, including statements as to the quality of post-transfer pension provision which was to be offered to the transferring employees by the transferee. The Court held that the quality of the post-transfer pension arrangements did not reflect the transferor's representations to the effect that they would be "broadly comparable" with the level of pension provision to which the transferring employees were entitled in respect of pre-transfer service, and thus found the transferor had made negligent misrepresentations. Liability for misrepresentations would normally have passed to the transferee as a consequence of the TUPE Regulations 1981; however, as the misrepresentations related to occupational pension schemes, the liability was held to be incapable of passing to the transferee due to the operation of the pensions exclusion and thus remained with the transferor.

3.2. The ECJ and Pensions Rights under TUPE

The issue of whether pension rights (or at least some pension rights) are capable of passing under TUPE (notwithstanding the decisions in the Warrener and Adams cases) was re-examined by the ECJ in 2002 in the case of *Beckmann v Dynamco Whicholoe Macfarlane*.[6] Mrs Beckmann was an

---

[4] See for instance Barber v. GRE [1990] 2 All ER 660 ECJ; Ten Oever v Stichting Bedrijfspensioenfonds Voor Het Glazenwassers [1993] PLR 317.

[5] Hagen v. ICI Chemicals and Polymers Ltd [2001 64 PBLR, 2001 ALL ER (D) 273 Oct]

[6] Beckmann v Dynamco Whicheloe Macfarlane Ltd [2002] IRLR 578 ECJ

employee of the National Health Service whose employment was transferred to Dynamco Whicholoe Macfarlane Ltd in 1995. In May 1997, she was made redundant, and a dispute arose as to whether she was entitled to certain benefits (payable as a result of redundancy) which had been provided under her old employer's pension scheme (the NHS pension scheme). The essential question was whether the relevant benefits (being an early retirement pension and certain lump sum benefits) were "old age benefits" (and therefore capable of falling within the scope of the pensions exclusion of the TUPE Regulations 1981) or not. The High Court referred this question to the ECJ. The ECJ considered the wording set out in Article 3(3) of the 1977 ARD, and concluded that as the general objective of the Articles 3(1) and 3(2) of the 1977 ARD is to safeguard the rights of employees in the event of transfers of undertakings, the exception contained in Article 3(3) must be interpreted strictly. The exception can therefore only apply to the types of benefits specifically listed in the exclusion, which must be construed in a narrow sense. In particular, in relation to the question before the Court, the ECJ determined that it is only benefits paid from the time that an employee reaches the end of his normal working life (as laid down by the governing provisions of the pension scheme in question) that can be classified as old age benefits.

Early retirement benefits and benefits intended to enhance the conditions of such retirement, paid in the event of dismissal to employees who have attained a specified age (for example, the benefits which were claimed by Mrs Beckmann) are not old age, invalidity or survivors' benefits under supplementary company or inter-company pension schemes within the meaning of Article 3(3) of the 1977 ARD. Such benefits do not, therefore, fall within the scope of the pensions exclusion under Article 3(3) (or the pensions exclusion set out in Regulation 7(1) of the TUPE Regulations 1981 derived from Article 3(3) or (after 6 April 2006) Regulation 10(1) of the TUPE Regulations 2006, and must, at least in principle, be capable of passing under TUPE.

It will be appreciated that one effect of the ECJ's ruling in the *Beckmann* case was to add to the uncertainty as to whether a transferee could become liable in relation to any pension rights enjoyed by a transferring employee under an occupational pension scheme before the TUPE transfer. This uncertainty was then further compounded by the ECJ in the following year as a result of its ruling in the case of *Martin v South Bank University*[7].

---

[7] Martin v. South Bank University (2003) PLR 199

The *Martin* case was brought by three nursing lecturers (Ms Martin, Mr Daby and Mr Willis) who were originally employed by the National Health Service, and who were active members of the NHS pension scheme. In November 1994, as part of a Government initiative to transfer nursing education into the higher education sector, the college in which they lectured became part of South Bank University. As a consequence, the applicants ceased to be eligible to accrue pension benefits under the NHS pension scheme; they instead were offered (and accepted) membership of the Teachers' superannuation scheme.

There were, however, significant differences between the benefits offered by the NHS pension scheme and those provided under the Teachers' superannuation scheme, particularly in respect of the benefits provided upon early retirement, with the benefits provided under the NHS pension scheme being the more generous.

In early 1997, two of the applicants (Ms Martin and Mr Daby) accepted offers of early retirement by the University which were made in response to anticipated Government cost-cutting proposals in respect of early retirement pensions. The University then contended that the applicants were entitled to the less generous early retirement benefits provided under the Teachers' superannuation scheme, rather than the terms which they would have received had they been retiring from service whilst active members of the NHS pension scheme. The applicants brought claims before the Croydon ET[8] which in turn referred a number of questions to the ECJ, essentially revolving around the central question of whether the applicants' rights in respect of early retirement benefits were capable of surviving the transfer of their employments to the University or whether the Article 3(3) of the ARD operated so as to preclude this.

The ECJ ruled:

1. Rights contingent upon dismissal or the grant of early retirement by agreement with the employer fall within the rights and obligations referred to in Article 3(1) of the 1977 ARD, and consequently fall within the scope of the Directive.
2. Early retirement benefits, and benefits intended to enhance the conditions of such retirement, paid in the event of early retirement

---

[8] Mr Willis remained an employee of the University but sought a declaration to the effect that if he ever became eligible for early retirement benefits, those benefits would be calculated on the terms of the NHS pension scheme, rather than those of the (less generous) Teachers' superannuation scheme.

arising by agreement between the employer and the employee, to employees who have attained a certain age, are not old age, invalidity or survivors' benefits under supplementary schemes within the meaning of Article 3(3) of the 1977 ARD. Article 3 of that directive is to be interpreted as meaning that obligations arising upon the grant of such early retirement, whether arising from a contract of employment, an employment relationship or a collective agreement binding the transferor as regards the employees concerned, are transferred to the transferee subject to the conditions and limitations laid down by Article 3, regardless of the fact that those obligations derive from statutory instruments (as was in fact the case in relation to the early retirement benefits provided under both the NHS pension scheme and the Teachers' superannuation scheme) or are implemented by such instruments and regardless of the practical arrangements adopted for such implementation.

3. Article 3 of the 1977 ARD precludes the transferee from offering the employees of a transferred entity terms less favourable than those offered to them by the transferor in respect of early retirement, and those employees from accepting those terms, where the purpose of offering such less favourable terms is to harmonise the terms of the transferring employees with those of the transferee's other employees at the time of the TUPE transfer unless the more favourable terms previously offered by the transferor arose from a collective agreement which is no longer legally binding on the transferring employees, having regard to the conditions set out in Article 3(2). (In this regard, the ECJ was reflecting the previous ruling in the case of *Daddy's Dance Hall*; however, in its reasoning justifying its rulings, the ECJ stressed that the 1977 ARD does not preclude an agreement by the transferring employees with the transferee to alter the employment relationship (whether in a manner unfavourable to the transferring employees or otherwise) insofar as such alterations are permitted by the applicable national law of the relevant member state in situations other than a transfer of an undertaking).

4. Where, in breach of the obligations imposed by Article 3 of the 1977 ARD, a transferee offers transferring employers early retirement terms which are less favourable than those to which they were entitled under their employment relationship with the transferor employer (and such employees accept early retirement), it is the legal responsibility of the transferee to ensure that those employees are accorded early retirement on the terms to which they were entitled under their employment relationship with their transferor. (Consequently, a transferee cannot

evade responsibility for honouring early retirement terms in a manner which is consistent with the transferring employees' rights which applied before the transfer date by arguing that the employees themselves have accepted less generous terms, thus confirming yet again the basic tenet of the ECJ's ruling in *Daddy's Dance Hall*).

The basic principle emerging from the *Beckmann* and *Martin* cases was and is simple to state: the TUPE pensions exclusion is not as comprehensive as was once thought; some occupational pension scheme obligations are capable, in principle, of passing from a transferor to a transferee, notwithstanding the existence of the exclusion. However, the implications of the ECJ's judgments in these cases were more difficult to describe comprehensively, and there remained many unanswered questions.

After a long hiatus, *Beckmann* and *Martin* issues again were considered by the Court in the case of *Procter & Gamble*.[9] This case (admittedly a first instance decision), involved the TUPE transfer of employees (who prior to the transfer had been active members of a pension scheme providing defined benefits), with the result that the relevant employees became deferred members of the transferor's pension scheme (and as a consequence, under the governing provisions of that scheme, no longer qualified for generous early retirement rights which were only available to active members of the scheme). The Court examined, and answered three questions:

1. Had the transferring members/employees rights and the transferring company obligations capable of being transferred under TUPE? The key issue here was an argument advanced by the transferor to the effect that the early retirement benefits were contingent on employer consents being granted. The transferor was under no contractual obligation to provide consent, and therefore (for TUPE purposes) no obligations in respect of such early retirement benefits passed under TUPE. The Court rejected this argument; the fact the early retirement rights may be contingent rights will not automatically prevent them from being capable of passing under TUPE.

2. What passes under TUPE – is it the liability for all early retirement rights or only the liability in respect of the early retirement rights that the transferring members/employees "lose" on becoming deferred pensioners under the transferor's scheme?

---

[9] Procter & Gamble Company v. Svenska Cellulosa Aletiebolaget SCA and another [2012] EWHC 1257 (Ch)

The Court held that the second answer was the correct answer –

"… any (but only) transferred rights or benefits comprised within [early retirement benefits] which have not already been met in economic substance by virtue of the transferring members becoming entitled to deferred pensions in the [transferor's scheme] will transfer…" One justification for this stance was the need to avoid a situation where the transferring members effectively receive at least an element of *"double pension"*.

3. What is the scope of Regulation 10(2) of the TUPE Regulations 2006 and the meaning of "old age benefits"? In this case, noting the wording of the pensions exclusion (and in particular the fact the "old age" benefits are caught by the exclusion), the Court effectively examined the question as to whether pension rights which are arguably characterised as early retirement rights (capable of passing under TUPE) retain that categorisation indefinitely, or only until normal pension date is achieved. (Or to adapt Mr Justice Hildyard's phrasing of the question: is it the case that *"once an early retirement benefit, never an old age benefit"*?)

The answer to the question was no: *"…instalments of pension paid to someone after [normal pension date] where the characteristic of the benefit and its obvious and only purpose has always been to support the recipient after retirement having attained a specified age and without any other trigger, fall to be characterised as old age benefits, and none the less simply because the pension had first come into payment before [normal pension date]."* Thus the transferee was liable (as a consequence of TUPE) only in respect of

(i.) the element(s) of early retirement rights which members had lost as a result of deferred pensioner status (referred to as "Enhancements" in the *Procter & Gamble*[10] case); and

(ii.) only in respect of benefits paid to the date of normal retirement.

The *Procter & Gamble* case, (unless later overruled) therefore, has to some extent clarified some of the aspects of *Beckmann* and *Martin* rights that were hitherto obscure. However, a number of issues are still unclear.

It is interesting to speculate, for example, whether any other pension scheme rights can be rights that are capable of being characterised as other than old age, survivors' or invalidity rights, and thus be capable (in principle) of not being "caught" by the pensions exclusion (i.e. capable of

---

[10] Procter & Gamble Company v. Svenska Cellulosa Aletiebolaget SCA and another [2012] EWHC 1257 (Ch)

being *"Beckmann/Martin-type"* rights). We may consider that in certain circumstances, late retirement benefits might be capable of being so construed, if they were ever held not to be old age benefits under supplementary company or inter-company pension schemes.

Following the original ECJ cases, it was suggested by certain commentators that the *Beckmann* and *Martin* cases are specific to their facts, or are only applicable to public sector schemes; after all, both cases involved transfers out of the NHS pension scheme. In practice, since then it has generally seemed unwise for any transferee to assume that this is the case; the ECJ rulings in these cases do not suggest that they are so limited and in the *Procter & Gamble* case the Court had no difficulty in applying the *Beckmann/Martin* principles to a private sector occupational pension scheme.

Further, it has been argued that employees seeking to claim *Beckmann/Martin*-type rights post-transfer must also accept that such rights are not necessarily absolute in nature (and the *Martin* ruling supports this argument); generally, such rights arise under the governing trust documentation of the transferor's occupational pension scheme, and invariably, such schemes are designed to be capable of amendment via the exercise of an amendment power set out in such documentation, and indeed to be capable of termination. It could, therefore, be argued (at least in some situations) that *Beckmann/Martin*-type rights can be subject to an implicit caveat that they are capable of being amended or terminated to the same extent as analogous benefit provisions under the transferor's pension scheme could be amended or terminated (though much would of course depend upon the exact nature of the amendment and/or termination powers set out under the governing provisions of the transferor's scheme). In some cases, such an argument may well have merit. However, when considering this point, it must be borne in mind that the exercise of a scheme's amendment power is generally subject to various restrictions and caveats, most notably those arising under section 67 of the Pensions Act 1995 – which effectively restricts the exercise of an amendment power in any manner which might adversely affect any entitlement, accrued right or pensions credit of any pension scheme unless various requirements are satisfied.

If, however, *Beckmann/Martin*-type rights arising under the transferor's pension scheme are themselves subject to an explicit caveat (for example, early retirement is permitted on an advantageous basis, but only with the prior written consent of the employer), then if those rights pass upon the making of a TUPE transfer, they must transfer subject to that caveat (in other words, the caveat also transfers). The *Beckmann* and *Martin* judgments do not permit transferring employees to "cherry pick" advantageous rights that are to pass upon the making of the TUPE transfer, whilst ignoring applicable restrictions.

Beckmann/Martin issues can pose problems when they arise in commercial transactions. Following the *Procter & Gamble* case, purchasers/acquirers of businesses involving a TUPE transfer from an employer operating a deferred benefit scheme will be keen to investigate the nature of any "enhancements" lost by transferring employees upon becoming deferred pensioners and for which the transferee employer may become liable (at least in respect of the period up to the normal date of retirement). Moreover, there will be a need to establish whether staff acquired in the past (whether as part of a "true" business acquisition or as a consequence of a share acquisition) were ever the subject of historic TUPE transfers, and whether they were ever members of pension schemes operated by former employers which created *Beckmann/Martin*-type obligations which still subsist and which could become the (direct or indirect) responsibility of the purchaser upon the completion of the transaction. In practice, so far as historic TUPE transfers are concerned it is unlikely in any but the simplest scenarios that a prospective purchaser will be able to obtain a satisfactorily comprehensive answer to any queries he may raise in this regard, and he may be obliged to rely on warranty and/or indemnity protection, assuming the prospective seller is willing to provide such protection (and assuming further, or course, that such protection is sufficiently robust so as to allow the purchaser to rely upon it in comfort).

It seems likely that (notwithstanding the *Procter & Gamble* case) the *Beckmann* and *Martin* cases will have the capability of complicating the negotiation of commercial transactions for some time to come. Further case law and/or new legislation (whether on a European or a domestic level) may help to clarify the position further.

It should be noted that Regulation 10(3) of the TUPE Regulations 2006 provides that an employee whose contract of employment is transferred in the circumstances described in Regulation 4(1) (i.e. under a TUPE transfer) shall not be entitled to bring a claim against his former (transferor) employer for breach of contract or constructive unfair dismissal under section 95(1)(c) of the ERA 1996 arising out of a loss or reduction in his rights under an occupational pension scheme in consequence of the TUPE transfer, save insofar as the alleged breach of contract or dismissal occurred before 6 April 2006. Consequently, it will be the transferee, rather than the transferor, who is potentially liable in respect of such claims arising as a result of any failure on its part to honour its pension obligations after that date.

The TUPE pension exclusion does not necessarily prevent the transfer of responsibility for discrimination claims from passing from a transferor to a transferee upon the occurrence of a TUPE transfer. This will be particularly relevant in relation to potential liabilities arising in respect of any failure by a transferor's pension scheme to fully equalise its retirement benefits as between male and female members as required in the light of the decisions of the ECJ in the "equality cases" of *Barber v GRE*[11], *Coloroll Pension Trustees Limited v Russell*[12] and related cases, and the equality provisions set out in sections 62 to 66 of the Pensions Act 1995.

3.3. Whitney v Monster Worldwide Ltd

Even if a particular right is excluded by the pensions exclusion, there may be other ways whereby it can pass to become an obligation of the transferee. This is demonstrated by the rulings of the High Court (and subsequently the Court of Appeal) in the case of *Whitney v Monster Worldwide Limited*[13].

The case concerned a group of employees who were members of a defined benefit occupational pension scheme; in 1989, it was closed to future accrual, and the employees were instead offered membership of a defined contribution occupational pension scheme in respect of future service. At the same time, (the Court subsequently held), they were offered by their employer ("MSL Group Ltd") a *"no-detriment"* guarantee (that is, effectively a (contractual) promise that their accrual of benefits under the replacement defined contribution schemes would be on no worse a basis than they would have enjoyed had they continued to accrue benefits under the defined benefit pension scheme. In February 1997, MSL Group Ltd (and the defined contribution pension scheme) was acquired by a purchaser (the existence of the no-detriment guarantee having been disclosed by the seller as part of the sale process); a few months later (in July 1997) the trading

---

[11] Barber v. GRE [1990] 2 All ER 660 ECJ

[12] Coloroll Pension Trustees Ltd v James Richard Russell, Daniel Mangham, Gerald Robert Parker, Robert Sharp, Joan Fuller, Judith Ann Broughton and Coloroll Group plc. (Social policy) [1994] ECJ C-200/91 (28 September 1994)

[13] Whitney v Monster Worldwide Limited [2009] EWHC 2993 (Ch); [2011004PBLR; [2010] EWCA Civ 1312]

business of MSL Group Ltd was transferred to another company within the purchaser's group (*"Monster Worldwide Ltd"*), and employees working within that business transferred to employment with Monster Worldwide Ltd by operation of the TUPE Regulations 1981.

At a later date, certain employees sought to enforce the no-detriment guarantee against Monster Worldwide Ltd.

Monster Worldwide Ltd attempted to argue that the no-detriment guarantee was not contractually effective (or that if it was, it was not effective against itself). Both the High Court and the Court of Appeal ruled that the guarantee had come into being as a contractual promise; however, the Court accepted that the guarantee was a term arising in connection with the claimant's employment relating to an occupational pension scheme and thus was excluded from the transfer as a consequence of the pensions exclusion. However, the Court also held that the obligation to honour the guarantee had passed to Monster Worldwide Ltd as a result of contractual novation (as a result of statements made to the transferring employees by the seller (and actions by the purchaser which could be construed as indicating it accepted that a novation of the rights and obligations relating to the no-detriment guarantee had taken place)). Monster Worldwide Ltd was thus required to honour the guarantee notwithstanding it was excluded from the TUPE transfer as a result of the pensions exclusion.

3.4.   Pensions and Public Sector Transfers

Public sector transfers represent another exception to the general operation of the exclusion. Before 14 June 1999, the pensions exclusion covered, broadly speaking, compulsory competitive tendering; however, on that date, the Government issued a press release announcing the extension (with immediate effect) of the protection awarded to public sector employees, emphasising that the protection applies to all Private Finance Initiatives and Public-Private Partnership contracts.

Essentially, there are two strands to this protection, covering past and future service pension rights. In respect of future service, the new (transferee) employer must offer broadly comparable pension provisions to those enjoyed by the transferring employees before the transfer, as assessed by the Government Actuary's Department. The Treasury has explained that this means there should be no identifiable employees who will suffer material detriment overall. If an individual will suffer as a result of a transfer, that individual must be awarded suitable compensation, for example, by means of a salary increase.

In order to protect the past service position, the Government requires that the new employer's replacement pension scheme must be prepared to accept a bulk transfer of accrued pension rights, and appropriate transfer credits must be provided.

An additional change to the pension aspects of outsourcing was introduced by the Government in January 2000 as a result of the publication of the Cabinet Office's *"Statement of Practice on Staff Transfers in the Public Sector"*. As a result of the Local Government Act 2003, compliance with this guidance effectively became a legal obligation for all *"best value local authorities"* (a class which is wider than simply local authorities, and including police authorities, fire authorities and similar groups) in England and Wales. These provisions essentially require that where the transferring employees are members of the Local Government Pension Scheme, they must be permitted following a transfer of their employment to continue to have access to a broadly comparable occupational pension scheme under which they can continue to accrue pension benefits in respect of future service. Contractors now have a choice of offering broadly comparable benefits under their own occupational pension arrangements, or gaining admitted body status under the Local Government Pension Scheme, meaning that the transferring employees' pension arrangements remain unchanged by the outsourcing.

3.5.   TUPE and the Pensions Act 2004

The Pensions Act 2004, ("PA 2004"), which received Royal Assent on 18 November 2004, with the majority of its provisions coming into force on 6 April 2005, introduced new measures of pension protection for transferring employees who are members of occupational pension schemes and who are subject to a TUPE transfer. These measures, set out in sections 257 and 258 of the PA 2004, and the Transfer of Employment (Pension Protection) Regulations 2005 (SI 2005/649) (the "Pension Protection Regulations"), have their origins in the December 1998 Green Paper issued by the Department of Social Security and entitled *A New Contract for Welfare - Partnership in Pensions*, in which the Government proposed that the scope of the protection afforded by TUPE should be extended to provide at least some measure of protection for transferring employees in relation to their occupational pension scheme rights. Various methods of achieving a degree of pension protection were considered and debated; eventually the Department of Trade and Industry issued a press release in February 2003 indicating that the issue of pension protection under TUPE would be considered separately from the general review of the operation of TUPE already discussed.

In June 2003, the Department of Work and Pensions issued its White Paper entitled *Simplicity, Security and Choice* in which it announced its proposals in relation to UK pensions reform; as part of those proposals the Government indicated that it intended to require transferees to provide at least a modicum of replacement pension provision for transferring employees who are the subject of a TUPE transfer. Those proposals subsequently took the form of sections 257 and 258 of the PA 2004, and the Pension Protection Regulations that came into force on 6 April 2005 (the "Pensions Protection Legislation").

Section 257(1) of the PA 2004 lays down the circumstances that must exist before the new pension protection requirements apply. Specifically:

(a) there must be a transfer of undertaking (or part of an undertaking) capable of constituting a TUPE transfer;

(b) as a consequence of the TUPE transfer, the (transferring) employees must cease to be employed by the transferor and instead become employed by the transferee; and

(c) immediately before the TUPE transfer occurs, the transferor must have participated in an occupational pension scheme, and the transferring employees must either have been:

    a. active members of the scheme (and if any of the benefits that may be provided under the scheme are money purchase benefits, the transferor must either be required to make employer contributions on behalf of those of the transferring employees who are active members of the scheme, or have previously made one or more such contributions even if not legally obliged to do so); or

    b. eligible to have become active members (and, if any of the benefits that may be provided under the scheme are money purchase benefits, the transferor must have been obliged to make employer contributions in respect of the transferring employees had they in fact been active members of the scheme); or

    c. be in a "membership waiting period" which (had they been able to complete the period but for the fact of the TUPE transfer) would upon its conclusion have enabled them either to become active members of the scheme or otherwise be eligible to become active members (and, again, if any of the benefits provided under the scheme are money purchase benefits, the transferor must have been obliged to make employer contributions in respect of the transferring employees had those employees in fact been active members of the scheme).

It has been observed (David Pollard in *Pensions and TUPE*, Industrial Law Journal vol. 34, No. 2, June 2005) that the PA 2004 does not clearly define the meaning of the term "eligible" as used in section 257 and that it is unclear as to whether the term only refers to situations where employees have an unfettered right of access to the pension scheme (which they may or may not choose to exercise), or whether it also covers situations where employee access requires the consent of, for example, the employer. Such conditions are often found in the governing provisions of pension schemes in respect of employees who have declined to join the scheme at the first opportunity. It would seem that the first interpretation is the most likely, but further clarification would be welcome.

Where the requirements of section 257(1) of the PA 2004 are met, and the transferee employer is thus under an obligation to provide a minimum level of replacement pension provision for the transferring employees, there are a number of options available to the transferee as specified under sections 258(2) and (3) of the PA 2004 and the Pension Protection Regulations. (In this regard, it should be noted that section 258(1) of the PA 2004 specifies that it is a condition of the transferring employees' contracts of employment with the transferee that sections 258(2) or (3) are complied with). Furthermore, it should be noted that the pension protection obligations are in addition to any liabilities which may pass to the transferee under the principles arising under the *Beckmann* and *Martin* cases.

The transferee can:

(a) ensure that, from the date of the TUPE transfer, the transferring employees are eligible to be active members of an occupational pension scheme in relation to which the transferee is a participating employer; or

(b) ensure that, from the date of the TUPE transfer, it either makes relevant contributions (which are discussed further below) to the stakeholder pension schemes of which the transferring employees are members or (if the transferring employees are not in fact members), it must offer to make relevant contributions to stakeholder pension schemes of which the transferring employees are eligible to be members (and not withdraw that offer).

If the transferee elects to provide an occupational pension scheme for the benefit of the transferring employees, there are further conditions that the transferee must satisfy. Section 258(2)(b) of the PA 2004 provides that if the scheme is a money purchase scheme, the transferee must make relevant contributions on behalf of those transferring employees who elect to become active members of the scheme. Alternatively, section 258(2)(c) of the PA 2004 provides that if the scheme is not a money purchase scheme, the transferee must either ensure that the pension scheme satisfies the statutory standard referred to in section 12A of the Pension Schemes Act 1993 or otherwise satisfy prescribed conditions (which are set out in the Pension Protection Regulations).

Regulation 2 of the Pension Protection Regulations currently provides that the transferee's pension scheme will satisfy the prescribed conditions if it provides either:

(a) for members to be entitled to benefits the value of which equals or exceeds 6% of pensionable pay for each year of employment (and it should be noted that the reference is not to each year of pensionable service) together with the total amount of any contributions made by the members, and, where members are required to make contributions to the scheme, for them to contribute at a rate which does not exceed 6% of their pensionable pay; or

(b) for the transferee employer to make relevant contributions to the scheme on behalf of each employee (and it should be noted that the reference is not to each transferring employee) who is an active member of the pension scheme.

It should be noted, however, that the Government has proposed changes to the minimal level of pension provision required under the Pensions Protection Legislation as a consequence of the introduction of the auto-enrolment regime. These changes are discussed in the next section.

Regulation 2(2) of the Pensions Protection Regulations defines a member's "pensionable pay" as being that part of the remuneration payable to a member of a pension scheme by reference to which the amount of contributions and benefits are determined under the rules of the scheme. Interestingly, neither the Pension Protection Regulations nor the PA 2004 specify how pensionable pay should be defined if the scheme's governing provisions provide differing definitions of pensionable pay for the purposes of calculating contribution rates and determining pension benefits (as in the case for some pension schemes). In practice, if this scenario is encountered, the transferee would be in compliance with the legislative requirements if it treats the members' pensionable pay as being the greater of their pay as defined for the purposes of calculating contribution rates and their pay as defined for benefit calculation purposes.

Regulation 3(1) provides that the transferee's contributions will be "relevant contributions" for the purposes of the legislation if:

(a) the contributions are made in respect of each period for which the employee is paid remuneration, provided that the employee also contributes to the pension scheme in respect of that period; and

(b) the amount contributed by the transferee in respect of each such period is at least equal to the amount contributed by the employee, provided that if the employee's contribution in respect of the relevant period equals or exceeds 6% of the employee's remuneration, the transferee is only obliged to contribute at a rate which is at least equal to 6% of the employee's remuneration.

In calculating the amount of an employee's remuneration for the purposes of Regulation 3(1), only gross basic pay (ignoring any pension contributions other than minimum payments within the meaning of the Pensions Schemes Act 1993 in relation to contracted-out pension schemes) is to be taken into account; no account is to be taken of bonuses, commission, payments, overtime or payments of a similar nature.

It should be noted that section 258(6) of the PA 2004 does allow the transferring employee(s) and the transferee to agree (at any time after the date of the TUPE transfer) to disapply the pension protection requirements, and agree to alternative pension arrangements of their own choosing.

3.6. TUPE and the Auto-enrolment Regime

The auto-enrolment regime, which is coming into effect in stages, starting in October 2012, requires employers to make arrangements for the auto-enrolment of eligible workers in pension schemes satisfying at least minimal criteria laid down under the auto-enrolment legislation (part 1 of the Pensions Act 2008 and underlying regulations); depending upon the type of scheme selected, the employer may also be required to make employer contributions to the scheme of (at least) a minimum rate specified under the legislation (eventually and broadly speaking, 3 per cent of a worker's "qualifying earnings" (i.e. earnings between upper and lower bands specified under the legislation)). If a transferee acquires transferring employees by operation of TUPE who would qualify as eligible workers under the auto-enrolment regime, the transferee would be obliged to ensure that any replacement scheme offered not only satisfied the requirements of sections 257 and 258 of PA 2004 and the Pension Protection Regulations but also was capable of being treated as a qualifying scheme for auto-enrolment purposes.

It should be noted that, following a consultation exercise in 2013, the Government has proposed changes to the Pensions Protection Legislation to address potential difficulties arising as a result of the interaction of the

TUPE and auto-enrolment regimes (and particularly the fact that, in certain circumstances, the application of the original pension protection legislation could lead to the pension provision of auto-enrolled members of defined contribution occupational pension schemes (operated on the basis of minimum auto-enrolment required contributions) being improved following a TUPE transfer, as a consequence of the obligation upon the new employer to provide access to replacement pension provision *at least* equal to the minimum standards prescribed by the Pensions Protection Legislation. To address this anomaly, the Government proposed that the Pension Protection Legislation should be amended so as to permit the transferee to choose to match (a) the contribution level chosen by the transferring employee (but limited to a cap of 6% of salary, or (b) the contributions made by the former employer (i.e. the transferor) immediately prior to the TUPE transfer. It was expected this change would come into force in October 2013, but at the time of writing (December 2013), the change has yet to be implemented. When considering the Pensions Protection Legislation it will, therefore, be important to check whether this (or a similar change) has yet been made.

Alternatively, if before the TUPE transfer, the transferring employees were members of stakeholder/personal pension schemes, to which the TUPE pensions exclusion (and the Pensions Protection Legislation) do not apply, any rights on the part of the transferring employees to have employer contributions paid in respect of them to a stakeholder/personal pension scheme at a particular rate would pass so as to become an obligation of the transferee, who would thus need to ensure that both the auto-enrolment requirements and the contractual obligations acquired as a result of the TUPE transfer are met.

In conclusion, there continues to be a pension exclusion under the new TUPE provisions capable of preventing the transfer of most (but not all) legal obligations (in respect of occupational pension schemes) from a transferor to a transferee upon the occurrence of a TUPE transfer. Despite the continued existence of the pension exclusion, *Beckmann/Martin*-type rights are capable of passing from one employer to another upon a TUPE transfer. There remains considerable uncertainty about the extent to which pensions rights are capable of being characterised as *Beckmann/Martin*-type rights, and often practical difficulties face a transferee who wishes to meet its obligations arising from the existence of such rights. Clarification of this important area of the law is needed and would assist in simplifying the negotiation of commercial transactions involving TUPE transfers. In addition, the PA 2004 imposes further obligations upon transferees, requiring them to provide at least a modicum of replacement pension provision for transferring employees in the private sector who enjoy access to an occupational pension scheme operated by the transferor immediately before the making of the TUPE transfer. However, such protection of future pension rights for transferring employees in the private sector contrasts unfavourably when compared to the more favourable protection afforded to employees transferring from or within the public sector and may be regarded as yet another factor distinguishing the pensions treatment of public sector workers as compared with those in the private sector.

4. TUPE AND INSOLVENCY

Times of economic downturn invariably lead to many insolvent transfers. Consequently, as both a sign of the times and a vexed area of law, this particular area has come under the judicial microscope in recent times.

The insolvency proceedings available in respect of companies are governed by the Insolvency Act 1986 as amended by the Enterprise Act 2002. The main types of insolvency proceedings which may be taken in respect of companies are liquidation (or winding up), whether effected under a court order, or voluntarily following a resolution passed by a general meeting of the company; company voluntary arrangements made by a company with its creditors (with or without approval of the court); and administration proceedings. The principal difference between these is that the main objective of liquidation (and possibly of company voluntary arrangements) is to realise and distribute the assets. Conversely, the purpose of an administration is to rescue the company as a going concern. Another insolvency device, available only to secured creditors, is a receivership, whereby the creditors may step in to realise their security to recover the secured amount without the company's affairs necessarily being wound up. In this chapter we assess the impact of insolvency law on business transfers, including recent rulings which have significantly impacted upon the insolvency law landscape when interfaced with TUPE.

4.1. The Old Regime

The 1977 ARD was silent as to the transfers of undertaking in an insolvency setting. The TUPE Regulations 1981 which gave effect to the 1977 ARD made any dismissal connected to the transfer, or which had the transfer as its principal reason, automatically unfair, unless it was for an "economic, technical or organisational" (ETO) reason. The effect was that a purchaser of an insolvent business bought with it the liabilities of the employment contracts and these could not be altered on a sale.

The resulting hazards (that the obligations imposed by ARD to transfer all employees on their current terms and conditions would act as a disincentive to the "rescue" of insolvent enterprise) were recognised by the ECJ at an early stage. In *Abels v Administrative Board of the Bedriftsvereniging voor Metaalindustrie en de Electrotechnische Industrie*[1], the ECJ attempted to distinguish between different types of insolvency proceedings in deciding

---

[1] Abels v. Administrative Board of the Bedrijfsverening [1985] ECR 469 ECJ

whether the Directive applies. It was here that ECJ first pronounced that *"It cannot be concluded that Directive no. 77/187 imposes on the Member States the obligation to extend the rules laid down therein to transfers of undertakings, businesses or parts of businesses taking place in the context of insolvency proceedings instituted with a view to the liquidation of the assets of the transferor under the supervision of the competent judicial authority."*[2]

The subsequent ECJ rulings in *D'Urso v Ercole Marelli Elettromeccanica SpA*[3] and *Spano v Fiat Goetch SpA*[4] clarified that the sale of an insolvent business as a going concern during administration proceedings that aims to rescue a business is within the scope of the Directive. In the UK, a similar legal approach was confirmed by the House of Lords Select Committee Report on the Amended Directive's proposals in 1996[5], as previously noted in Chapter 2.

In *D'Urso*, the insolvent transferor was in 'special administration' proceedings under Italian law on compulsory liquidation of large undertakings in financial difficulties. The ECJ identified two distinct types of procedure available under Italian law within the framework of 'special administration'. The first type of procedure had the same effect in substance as liquidation; the second type allowed the undertaking to continue trading under the direction of a court-appointed administrator. The latter procedure was held by the ECJ to be within the scope of 1997 ARD's application. In *Spano*, the case which also examined special administration proceedings under Italian law, the ECJ found that the purpose of a declaration that an undertaking is in financial difficulties is to enable it to improve its economic and financial situation and above all to preserve jobs. The ECJ observed that an undertaking found to be in financial difficulties is subject to a procedure which, far from being aimed at the liquidation of the undertaking, is designed to promote the continuation of its business. It was held that the economic and social objectives pursued by procedures of this type could not explain or justify the circumstances where, when all or part of the undertaking concerned is transferred, its employees lose the rights which the ARD confers on them.

---

[2] Abels at para 2

[3] D'Urso v. Ercole Marelli Elettromeccanica Spa [1992] IRLR 136 ECJ

[4] Spano v. Fiat Geotch SpA [1996], C-427/93, IDS Brief 558, ECJ

[5] H.L. Paper 38, 13 February 1996 (see S Hardy and R Painter, *"Revising the Acquired Rights Directive"* 1996 25 I.L.J. 160-1685).

The insolvency exception continued to be advanced in *Jules Dethier Equipement SA v Dassy[6]*. Here the plaintiff employee was dismissed by the court-appointed liquidator of a Belgian enterprise, Sovam SPRL. Following the dismissal, the assets of Sovam were transferred to another company, Dethier. The employee asserted claims for sums due to him by way of compensation in lieu of notice, accrued holiday leave and bonuses against his former employer, Sovam and against Dethier. He contended that the transfer constituted a 'contractual transfer' within the meaning of the Belgian legislation implementing the ARD.

The ECJ examined the procedure for liquidation of a company under Belgian law and found that it involved the steps which, following dissolution of a commercial company, were aimed at paying creditors out of the corporate assets and distributing any balance to the members. The same procedure applied regardless of the reason for dissolution. During the liquidation, the company acted through the liquidator who represented it vis-à-vis third parties. Under the law, the liquidators were appointed either under the articles of association or by general meeting. If the general meeting did not agree on a candidate by the requisite majority, a liquidator would be appointed by the court. In the latter event, the liquidation was conducted under court supervision, as it was in this case. The only difference from voluntary liquidation was that the procedure for appointing a liquidator was different.

The ECJ ruled that the determining factor is the purpose of the procedures in question although account should also be taken of the form of the procedure, in so far as it means that the undertaking continues or ceases trading. The criterion relating to the purpose of the procedure for winding up by the court, in the instant case, was not conclusive, since the liquidation proceedings could be used to bring a company's activities to an end whatever the reason for that course. From the form of the procedure, however, it was apparent that the liquidator, although appointed by the court, was acting on behalf of the company in selling its assets and under the supervision of the general meeting. It was held that the ARD 1977 (77/187/EEC) applied to a transfer of an undertaking being wound up by a court through a liquidator if the undertaking continues to trade while it is being wound up.

The TUPE Regulations 1981 initially attempted to address the original (1977) ARD's lack of insolvency provisions by introducing the concept of

---

[6] Jules Dethier Equipement SA v Dassy and anor ECJ Case C-319/94 [1998] IRLR 266

"hiving-down" for business transfers by receivers or liquidators. Regulation 4 provided that where a receiver, administrator or liquidator transferred from an insolvent company part or all of that company's business to a wholly owned subsidiary – in other words, hiving down – there was no relevant transfer at that stage and the operation of TUPE was effectively suspended until such time as another party acquired the subsidiary by share transfer or purchased the undertaking as a going concern.

The purpose of this provision was to promote the sale of insolvent businesses by allowing for the employees, and any debts toward them, to remain the responsibility of the insolvent parent company. The usual hiving-down arrangement is that the receiver or liquidator transfers the business but not the employees, to a subsidiary company. In practice, this led to employees being dismissed after the hiving down. This approach was first upheld in *Secretary of State for Employment v Spence*, a case involving a transferor in receivership. Here the entire workforce of Spence and Sons was dismissed some three hours before an agreement was reached with the purchaser to acquire plant, stock, work in progress, intangible assets and goodwill of the company. Having found that the workforce was dismissed, the new owners considered whether to dispose of the assets of the business for cash, to move the business to one of their other factories or to maintain the business as a going concern. In the end, they decided on the last option and the workforce was re-employed the following morning under new contracts of employment. The Court of Appeal held that where employees were dismissed hours before the transfer the continuity of their employment was not preserved by TUPE and that, in order to pass, the employment contract had to actually subsist at the moment of the transfer. The court's reasoning was based on the narrow construction of Regulation 5(3) which referred to persons employed "immediately before the transfer".

The practice of dismissing the workforce in a hive-down effectively ended after the House of Lords' decision in *Litster v Forth Dry Dock and Engineering Company Ltd*, previously discussed in Chapter 2, which made it clear that where employees are dismissed by reason of a relevant transfer the transferor's debts toward them still pass to the transferee even if the dismissals took place in advance of the transfer. In *Litster*, the receivers agreed to sell the business assets to the transferee and one hour before the transfer took place the workforce were told by the receivers that the business was to close down, they were dismissed with immediate effect, and that no further funds were available to pay their wages and no payments would be made for accrued holiday pay or for the period of notice. Only three former employees of the transferor were taken on by the transferee who preferred to recruit elsewhere at lower rates of pay. The House of Lords considered whether TUPE properly implemented the 1977 ARD. It was held that in order to fully implement the ARD, additional words had to be read into Regulation 5(3) of the TUPE Regulations 1981 as follows: *"a person so employed immediately before the transfer or [who] would have been so employed if he had not been unfairly dismissed in circumstances described in Regulation 8(1)"*. Former Regulation 8(1) of the TUPE Regulations 1981 rendered dismissals connected with the transfer automatically unfair if the transfer or a reason connected with it is the reason or principal reason for the dismissal.

The High Court confirmed in its judgment in *Re Maxwell Fleet and Facilities Management Ltd (in administration) (No. 2)*[7] that the *Litster* approach extends to hiving down cases. Here the parties agreed to transfer the business by means of a series of transactions agreed on the same date. Under the first transaction, the administrators of Maxwell agreed to sell the business to Dancequote, an off-the-shelf company whose shares were held by the administrators. The agreement provided that Dancequote would not employ Maxwell's employees. In the second transaction, Dancequote agreed to sell its business to Fleet and Distribution Management Ltd. By those means, the parties hoped to take advantage of Regulation 4 of the TUPE Regulations 1981. The issue arose as to whether Regulation 4 should be given a construction which defeated attempts to circumvent the purpose of the ARD in safeguarding employees' rights on transfer. The court applied *Litster* principles and held that on its true construction Regulation 4 did not prevent the transfer of employees' liabilities to the ultimate transferee, although the transaction in question was not part of an orthodox hive down. The court observed that:

"Regulation 4, although not specifically envisaged by the directive, enables the purpose of the directive to be achieved while permitting a business hived down to a subsidiary as is so frequently the case in English insolvencies. The purpose of the hiving down is achieved and the relevant transfer postponed (not cancelled) to meet the objective of the directive in passing responsibility for these employee liabilities to the ultimate transferee. There would otherwise be risks including that of the intermediary subsidiary created by the administrators being left with

---

[7] Re Maxwell Fleet and Facilities Management Ltd (in administration) (No. 2) [2001] 1 WLR 323

responsibilities which the directive intended should rest with the transferee, not the asset-less intermediary."[8]

4.2. "Hiving-down"

The "hiving-down" provision rightly disappears in the TUPE Regulations 2006. As stated in the consultation paper[9], in the light of the *Litster* judgment, and the Government's intention to take advantage of the two new optional derogations in Article 5.2 of the Directive (see discussion below), the existing provision relating to hiving down no longer serves any useful purpose.

In addition to the hiving down carve-out, some flexibility to insolvent employers was afforded by Regulation 8(2) of the TUPE Regulations 1981 which permitted dismissals and changes to terms and conditions to be made for 'economic, technical or organisational reasons entailing changes in the workforce' (ETO reasons). The meaning of ETO in the insolvency setting has never been very clear. There has been considerable confusion as to when a change is for an ETO reason or for a reason connected to the transfer, which is not permitted under TUPE.

4.3. The meaning of ETO in insolvency situations

The meaning of ETO has been interpreted by the courts as relating to the conduct of the business. In *Wheeler v. Patel*[10], where the EAT stated that a desire to obtain an enhanced price for the business or to achieve a sale was unrelated to the conduct of business and, therefore, not an "economic" reason for the purposes of Regulation 8(2) of the TUPE Regulations 1981. The EAT went further to criticise the view expressed by the Scottish EAT in *Anderson v Dalkeith Engineering Ltd*[11] that where an employee is dismissed by the transferor at the insistence if the transferee, the reason for the dismissal is "economic". The holding in *Wheeler v Patel*, undoubtedly, created considerable difficulties for insolvency practitioners where the ultimate objective was for a business to be sold as a going concern.

---

[8] At p. 869.

[9] *Transfer of Undertakings (Protection of Employment) Regulations 1981 (1981/1794), Government Proposals for Reform*, Detailed Background Paper (September 2001)

[10] Wheeler v. Patel [1987] IRLR 211 EAT

[11] Anderson v. Dalkeith Engineering [1980] ICR 66 CA

The relationship of ETO to the conduct of business was revisited in *Thompson v SCS Consulting Ltd*[12]. Here the EAT emphasised that an employment tribunal *"must consider whether the reason was connected with the future conduct of the business as a going concern"* in deciding whether the ETO is the principal reason for dismissal. The EAT affirmed the tribunal's decision and held that it was entitled to take into account as relevant evidence of whether there was any collusion between the transferor and transferee in relation to the dismissals and whether the transferor or those acting on its behalf had any funds to carry on the business or any business at the time of the decision to dismiss.

In a series of EAT decisions a finding of whether or not dismissals were related to the transfer seemed to hinge on the timing of these dismissals. Where the dismissals occurred shortly before the transfer took place they were found to be connected with transfers. Conversely, where there was a longer gap, the chances of a causal link being established were reduced.

One of such cases was *Ibex Trading Co Ltd v Walton*[13] where claimant employees were dismissed on 16 October 1991 (with effect from 4 November). On 11 November an offer to purchase the business was made, which ultimately led to a purchase on 13 February 1992. The EAT affirmed the ruling of the industrial tribunal that the employees had not been dismissed by reason of *"the transfer or a reason connected with it"* within the meaning of Regulation 8(1). The holding emphasised that although it is not always necessary for the prospective transferee to be identified, since sometimes one purchaser replaces another at the last minute, *"in the present case, at the stage of dismissal, a transfer was a mere twinkle in the eye and might never have occurred"*[14].

A strikingly different conclusion was reached in *Harrison Bowden Ltd v Bowden*[15]. Here the administrative receivers of a company which had employed the claimant employee for two and a half years advertised the sale of the business as a going concern. The following day, the receivers dismissed most of the workforce, including the complainant. EAT held that although there was no specific identifiable transferee employer at the

---

[12] Thompson v SCS Consulting Ltd & Ors [2001] EAT 34/00

[13] Ibex Trading Co Ltd. v Walton & Others [1994] IRLR 564 EAT

[14] See Kerry Foods v. Creber [2000] IRLR 10 EAT for a case involving a short gap and an analysis of Regulation 8(1) and (2).

[15] Harrison Bowden Ltd v. Bowden [1994] ICR 186 EAT

moment of the dismissal, the complainant was dismissed in connection with the transfer for the purpose of regulation 8(1). More recently, in *Morris v John Grose Group Ltd*[16] the EAT expressly stated that it preferred the decision in *Harrison Bowden* to that in *Ibex Trading*.

Following *Harrison Bowden* the EAT took an even wider approach to transfer related dismissals in *Michael Peters Ltd v Farnfield (in administrative receivership)*[17]. Even though there was no evidence that the dismissal was connected with a particular transfer, the EAT upheld the employment tribunal's decision that dismissals were connected with the eventual transfer as they were deemed necessary to achieve the sale of the business. Mention was made of the fact that the transfer of a business was the ultimate objective of an administration or a receivership. Guidance given by the Court of Appeal in *Dynamex Friction Limited & Others v. AMICUS*[18], held that in determining whether the reason for dismissal was economic where an administrator had been the voice and mind of the employer in effecting those dismissals, it was the administrator's reasoning that was crucial.

The ETO exception continues in the TUPE Regulations 2006 under Regulation 4(5). These Regulations, however, neither expand on the meaning of the term 'economic, technical or organisational' nor provide a list of specimen reasons that would fall within this definition.

4.4.   Insolvency under the 2006 regime & beyond

Quite despairingly, the 2014 TUPE Amendment Regulations do not amend the pre-existing provisons relating to TUPE in insolvency situations. As a result, the insolvency provisions of the 2006 TUPE regime remain intact and are contained in Regulations 8 and 9 of the TUPE Regulations 2006. Regulation 8 excludes certain insolvency proceedings from the application of the provisions on transfer related liabilities and unfair dismissal, and spells out where the liability for pre-existing debts to employees falls. Under Regulation 9, the variations to terms and conditions of employment in connection with transfers of insolvent businesses will become valid subject to certain safeguards aimed at employee protection.

Article 5.1 of the revised ARD (reflecting case law on the original Directive discussed above, in particular, the ECJ's decision in *Abels*) states that unless

---

[16] Morris v John Grose Group Ltd [1998] EAT 773/97

[17] Michael Peters Ltd v. Farfield [1995] IRLR 190 EAT

[18] Dynamex Friction Limited & Others v. AMICUS [2008] IRLR 515

Member States provide otherwise, the normal safeguards for employees against transfer-related changes to terms and conditions and transfer related dismissals do not apply where *"the transferor is the subject of bankruptcy proceedings or any analogous insolvency proceedings which have been instituted with a view to the liquidation of the assets of the transferor and are under the supervision of a competent public authority (which may be an insolvency practitioner authorised by a competent public authority)."*

The Insolvency Act 1986 imposes a requirement that persons who fulfil the principal functions in the administration of the debtor's assets in all types of insolvency proceedings should be professionally qualified and authorised as insolvency practitioners. Consequently, procedures available under the Insolvency Act 1986 and excluded from the application of the ARD under Article 5.1 will be those that have liquidation of the assets of the insolvent enterprise as their main purpose. Procedures that fall within this description will include compulsory winding-up and bankruptcy, and, possibly, also creditors' voluntary winding-ups. Article 5.1 is reflected in Regulation 8(7), the net effect being that where the transferor is the subject of the Article 5.1 proceedings no liability will transfer at all, and the provisions relating to automatic unfair dismissal will not apply.

With relation to other types of insolvency proceedings, Article 5.2 of the revised ARD gives Member States two options in cases where its requirements are applied in relation *"insolvency proceedings . . . under the supervision of a competent public authority (which may be an insolvency practitioner determined by national law)"*. The first option is to provide that the transferor's pre-existing debts toward the employees do not pass to the transferee in cases giving rise to protection for employees at least equivalent to that covered by the EC Insolvency Payments Directive (80/987/EEC). The second option is to allow employers and employee representatives to agree changes to terms and conditions of employment by reason of the transfer itself, provided that this is done in accordance with national law and practice and with a view to ensuring the survival of the business and thereby preserving jobs (just as they can in cases of insolvency where no TUPE transfer is involved).

The underlying aim of these options is to allow Member States to promote the sale of insolvent businesses as going concerns. The consultation document which preceded the TUPE Regulations 2006 pointed out that this aim is in line with the "rescue culture" that the UK Government aims to promote. The Regulations take advantage of both of these options.

The effect of Regulation 8 is that in relevant insolvency proceedings the transferor's pre-existing debts toward relevant employees that were within the categories and statutory upper limits on amounts guaranteed under Part XII of the ERA 1996 (and equivalent Northern Ireland provisions) would fall to be met not, as at present, by the transferee but by the National Insurance Fund (with the Secretary of State becoming a creditor by subrogation in the insolvency proceedings). In respect of debts over and above those that could be met from the National Insurance Fund, the new Regulations provide that they pass to the transferee as under the old law.

Part XII of the ERA 1996 protects minimum guaranteed payments to employees of employers who have become insolvent. Under the old law, these payments were usually only available when employment was terminated due to an insolvency which meant that they would only apply if the employees were dismissed by the transferor (see section 182(b) of the EReLA 1999). Regulation 8(3) deems employees' contracts to have been terminated, with the date of the transfer treated as the date of termination in order to entitle them to statutory assistance. This will allow the dismissed employees to claim from the National Insurance Fund for arrears in pay, any period of notice, holiday pay and any entitlement to the basic award of compensation for unfair dismissal, and so relieve the transferee of these expenses.

Regulation 8(2) defines a relevant employee as being an employee of the transferor whose employment contract passes from the transferor to the transferee by virtue of the operation of the TUPE Regulations 2006 in relation to the relevant transfer, or whose employment contract is terminated before the relevant transfer in the circumstances described in Regulation 7(1), as discussed in Chapter 6.

Regulation 8(6) defines relevant insolvency proceedings as meaning insolvency proceedings which have been opened in relation to the transferor employer but not with a view to the liquidation of the assets of the transferor and which are under the supervision of an insolvency practitioner.

At the EAT, the then President Elias J, in *Secretary of State for DTI v. Slater*[19] held that Regulation 8(6) applied where the insolvent business was being liquidated. However, insolvency proceedings had to be in place when the business transferred and had to be subject to the supervision of an

---

[19] Secretary of State for DTI v. Slater [2008] ICR 54

insolvency practitioner. Consequently, in order to fulfil the requirements of both Regulations 8(6) and 8(7), an insolvency practitioner, as defined in section 388 of the Insolvency Act 1986, had to be appointed at the time of the transfer. Further, even if there were insolvency proceedings in place when the business was transferred, they had to be under the supervision of an insolvency practitioner. In this case, since they were not under the supervision of an insolvency practitioner, albeit a creditors' voluntary liquidation had occurred, no insolvency practitioner had been appointed so as to supervise the insolvency proceedings. Therefore, the liability for debts did not lie with the Secretary of State.

4.5.   Pre-Pack insolvency

Pre-pack insolvency has come of age since 2005. Early sales of businesses in administration are common in turbulent economic times. The Statement of Insolvency Practice 16 on pre-packs, which came into force on 1 January 2009, places the legitimacy of such an insolvency approach beyond doubt. Such is clearly enhanced by the decision of the EAT in *Oakland v. Wellswood (Yorkshire) Ltd*[20], where it was held that TUPE did not apply, by way of Regulation 8(7) where insolvency proceedings had been instituted with a view to liquidation of assets.

This case highlights Parliament's failure to specify which particular insolvency proceedings were to be considered as instituted with a view to liquidation of assets. Further, Government guidance was criticised by HHJ Clark as unhelpful, albeit it suggested that the TUPE exception would not apply to an administration. Oakland found it was possible to distinguish between two types of administration: one with a view of re-stabilising the business as a going concern and one where there is no intention to operate/trade the business. Clearly, whilst Article 5(2) of the ARD provides for individual Member States' governments to list which insolvency proceedings amount to a sale as a going concern (in contrast to the converse a business closure) such a step had not be taken by the UK Government.

In contrast, in *OTG v. Barke*,[21] Underhill J (then President) held that administration proceedings under the Insolvency Act 1986 Sch.B1 were not capable of constituting *"bankruptcy ... or ... analogous insolvency proceedings which have been instituted with a view to the liquidation of the assets of the*

[20] Oakland v. Wellswood (Yorkshire) Ltd [2009]

[21] OTG v. Barke [2011] ICR 781

transferor" within the meaning of the Regulation 8(7) TUPE 2006. However, the Court of Appeal, in an attempt to clarify matters, in *Key2Law (Surrey) LLP V. De'Antiquis*[22], Rimer LJ giving the leading judgment, upheld the Employment Appeal Tribunal that administration proceedings under the Insolvency Act 1986 Sch.B1 could not constitute *"insolvency proceedings which have been instituted with a view to the liquidation of the assets of the transferor."* Accordingly, Regulation 8(7) is to be utilised in narrow circumstances.

4.6. Permitted variations of terms and conditions of employment

Regulation 9(1) provides that where insolvency proceeding within the Article 5.2 derogation have been opened in respect of the transferor, changes by reason of the transfer itself (that is, changes for which there is no ETO reason that would render them potentially valid) may be lawfully made to the terms and conditions of employment of affected employees provided certain conditions are met.

This effectively allows employers and employee representatives the same freedom to negotiate in transfer cases as in other cases where changes to terms and conditions may be agreed with a view to securing the survival of an insolvent business and the consequent saving of jobs.

The safeguards in Regulation 9 (in respect of TUPE transfers made and variations agreed on or after 31 January 2014) are, first, that the changes should be agreed between either the transferor or the transferee, on the one side, and appropriate representatives of the affected employees, on the other. Secondly, the variations to the terms must be designed to safeguard employment opportunities by ensuring the survival of the undertaking or business or part of the undertaking or business. Lastly, the sole or principal reason for the variation must be the transfer itself and not a reason referred to in Regulation 4(5)(a). The latter two form the definition of "permitted variations" set out in Regulation 9(7) (as amended by the 2014 TUPE Amendment Regulations).

It is not entirely clear what is meant by *"ensuring the survival of the undertaking"*. Presumably, it will be the transferee who will decide what changes to the employment terms are required in order to rescue the undertaking. There is no standard by which to judge apart from what terms would be required to persuade the transferee to enter into a rescue

---

[22] Key2Law (Surrey) LLP V. De'Antiquis [2011] EWCA Civ 1567

plan. Moreover, it is doubtful that employees would have any bargaining power at all in such circumstances.

The definition of appropriate representative used for the purposes of this Regulation (see Regulation 9(2)) is consistent with that used for information and consultation purposes in Regulation 10 of the TUPE Regulations 1981. In essence, if there is an independent trade union recognised for collective bargaining purposes, the appropriate representative is a representative of that trade union. In any other case, the appropriate representatives should be appointed or elected by affected employees. To be valid, the appointment and authority of these representatives must satisfy detailed requirements.

In non-union cases, in order for the agreement to be effective in varying the contracts of employment of the individual employees represented, it must be in writing and the employer must have to have given the employees in question the text of the variation(s) in advance of it coming into effect, along with such guidance as they might reasonably require in order to understand fully the proposed changes.

Under the TUPE Regulations 2006, representatives for the purposes of agreeing changes to terms and conditions are given rights equivalent to those enjoyed by representatives for information and consultation purposes. Those who participate in the election of such representatives are also given equivalent rights. The same individuals can potentially act as representatives for both purposes, provided that, in non-union cases, they have authority from their constituent employees in both respects.

The new provisions are expected to give employers the confidence to negotiate changes to terms and conditions, reduce transactional costs associated with transfers in insolvency, reduce perceived legal risks, and potentially improve business efficiency. They will reduce the incentive for employers to make transfer-related dismissals in order to be able to offer the employees re-engagement on new terms and conditions, and then rely on the ETO defence in any resulting unfair dismissal claims.

One major problem for those involved in the negotiations with employees is likely to be that of tight time constraints. Insolvency situations often require quick action in order to rescue an enterprise. The Society of Insolvency Practitioners, in their evidence to the House of Lords

Committee[23] stated that *"Although Insolvency Practitioners like to observe consultation procedures, whenever possible, it needs to be recognised that in most cases it will simply not be practicable to comply with the requirements of the Directive"*. The reason for this is *"the very tight timescales"* in which the decisions affecting the future of the workforce are taken. This may also create a problem, as the insolvency practitioner owes a duty to the creditors which may at times conflict with the duties to protect the interests of employees under the Regulations.

The TUPE Regulations 2006 already have a requirement for consultation with appropriate representatives in the event of a proposed TUPE transfer. The additional consultation requirements (set out in Regulation 9 of the TUPE Regulations 2006), which must be satisfied in order to change terms and conditions in the context of relevant insolvency proceedings, will add to the worries of those concerned with the rescue on the management side and of the affected employees. This will be the case where, for example, there is no trade union and employees would need to elect the representatives before the consultation can begin. In some cases, the employees will decline to become involved in such a process. It is unclear whether, under the Regulations, it is permissible for the employer to simply provide information to affected employees, or whether, in these circumstances, it will not be possible to vary the terms at all.

4.7.   Notification requirements

Another point of which insolvency practitioners should be mindful is the new notification requirements upon the transferor with regards to the rights and liabilities of transferring employees. Article 3(2) of the ARD 2001 allows Member States to oblige transferors to notify transferees of employment rights and obligations which are or ought to have been known to the transferor at the time of transfer. Regulation 11 implements this option, as discussed in Chapter 6.

4.8.   Misuse of insolvency proceedings

The amended Directive requires Member States to *"take appropriate measures with a view to preventing misuse of insolvency proceedings in such a way as to deprive employees of the rights provided for in this Directive"*.

This represents a concern that employers could "engineer" insolvency situations in order to allow transfers to take place outside the scope of the

---

[23] Written evidence to the House of Lords Select Committee on the European Communities, session 1995-1996, 5th Report.

TUPE Regulations 2006 or to make use of the new more flexible approach adopted in the draft new rules on insolvency transfers. The Government has decided that the existing safeguards contained in the Insolvency Act 1986 and the Company Directors' Disqualification Act 1986, as amended by the Insolvency Act 2000, are sufficient to provide the safeguards required by the Directive and, consequently, no new amendments to the TUPE legislation have been made in that regard.

4.9. Insolvency and TUPE Working Together?

The intended benefit of the TUPE Regulations 2006 was to revive the rescue culture, and the encouragement of transfers of insolvent businesses to begin afresh under different employers rather than their closures and liquidations, with inevitable redundancies of their workers. Notwithstanding this, all the existing case law relating to TUPE transfers continues still to apply the TUPE Regulations 2006.

Insolvency practitioners will now have the choice between, on the one hand, closing the business applying redundancy law, and perhaps leaving it for the transferee to re-engage employees on different terms, or, on the other hand, rescuing the business by re-negotiating with employees under the provisions contained in Regulations 9. One hurdle in relation to the latter option may be the need for the insolvency proceedings to be handled quickly. Whichever option is selected, recent case law highlights that the insolvency practitioner's intentions are crucial to the question of the applicability of TUPE. Moreover, when subject to the supervision of an insolvency practitioner, there is danger that prolonged negotiations for a variation of the terms of employment may prove a less attractive option when a business is threatened with insolvency.

Thus far, the TUPE Regulations 2006 have been shown to have missed the opportunity to spell out exactly which insolvency proceedings fall within the scope of Regulation 8(6) and which are exempt under Regulation 8(7). The likely effect of this is that disputes over this issue will continue where negotiations of new terms fail or are not practical and the insolvency practitioners choose to dismiss the entire workforce; and associated costs to insolvent businesses (including the costs of contesting court and tribunal cases) will be incurred.

Clearly, the TUPE Regulations 2006 have not been able to prevent administrations from turning into liquidations in every case, but there remains hope that the specific insolvency provisions will mean that more insolvent businesses are capable of being rescued and thereby more jobs (or just some) preserved. Even so, it is increasingly clear is that the Insolvency

Act 1986 is in need of some modernisation to meet the demands of the new TUPE Regime of 2006. It is therefore likely that the *Oakland/OTG/ De'Antiquis* saga will continue.

5. SERVICE PROVISION CHANGES AND TUPE

Now that the legal framework concerning business transfers has been cast, this guide considers the policy that constantly challenges the TUPE framework. In the previous chapters numerous references have been made to outsourcing (contracting-out, contracting-in – "service provision changes" or "SPC", to adopt the new phraseology contained in the revised TUPE Regulations 2006). It is this policy shift that has complicated TUPE more than perhaps any other issue and, since its innovation in 2006, has cluttered the caselaw with inconsistent rulings.

Until 1980 the legal regimes of the public and private sectors within the UK were distinctly different. Since the advent of contracting-out which, as the term is used in this context, is not to be confused with outsourcing, the legal regime has recast the public sector more closely to the private sector model. This chapter seeks to introduce and explain contracting-out and its impact upon TUPE. The law relating to business transfers in the UK presents a new problem when applied to contracting-out, as to whether, or not, outsourcing exercises amount to a business transfer.

5.1. What is service provision change (aka 'out-sourcing')?

The public sector in the UK is now subject to a regime of contracting out and market testing of various functions to external service providers. It should be noted that UK government policy has asserted that contracting-out in the public sector "ensures that competition is both free and fair". Contracting-out therefore seeks to increase the effectiveness of market forces, in bringing about improved quality and cost-effectiveness by means of direct and indirect competition. In a global context, from 1960-90 the largest growth in the public sector occurred within the EU, whilst it had been moderate in the US. Three factors were highlighted as important when considering the public sector in a global context, wages, flexibility and mobility. In the preface to the UK government's 'Market Testing Guidance', the then Secretary of State, William Waldegrave MP, asserted that:

"Market testing is helping to improve the quality and the cost-effectiveness of many activities...In promoting the extension of market testing and competitive tendering we are endeavouring to ensure that competition is both free and fair".

Market testing has many forms. Generally, market testing is the subjection of public services to the discipline of the market. The various forms of market testing include facilities management; management buy-out;

formerly Compulsory Competitive Tendering (CCT) , and now 'Best Value'/outsourcing ("service provision changes"). Contracting-out was in the 1980s and 1990s the most common and widely-used form of market testing. The bedrock foundation of contracting-out is a belief in the merits of free markets. The rationale behind contracting-out is that the provision of services in the public sector lacks competitive pressures which ensure efficient provision. From the outset is important to distinguish contracting-out from privatisation. Privatisation concerns the situation where the assets involved in a service are directly transferred to private ownership. In contrast, contracting-out concerns the ideal of cost reduction in the provision of services in the public sector. Contracting-out is a process by which contractors compete with each other in an attempt to be awarded a particular contract.

Whether contracting-out is adopted or not, contractor failure remains a common feature of UK service provision, whether public or private. Contractor failure can be defined as a situation where a contractor fails to attain the service delivery standard previously agreed. Often the contractors become bankrupt and the service is not provided at all. One potential solution to this problem is the usage of performance bonds. Performance bonds are guarantees which safeguard against contractor failure. These bonds (which are effectively indemnities) are given so that if the contractor fails to attain the service standard agreed, then the bond can be used to finance the ensuing retendering exercise. The so-called 'Contractor Specification' in the tendering process which translates the policy decision into service requirements by setting overall service objectives establishes the importance of such indemnities. This specification ensures that when bids are submitted they include performance bonds guaranteeing agreed quality levels of service delivery.

5.2.   Workforce matters in local authority contracts: Best Value

The Office of Government Commerce (OGC)'s Code of Practice on Workforce Matters in the Public Sector Service Contracts (CoP), applicable to all local authorities since 2 April 2003, sets out the approach to workforce matters which involve a transfer of staff from local authorities to service providers.

Of paramount importance is the fact that the CoP recognises: *"that there is no conflict between good employment practice, value for money and quality of service"*. The CoP affirms that it is the intention that all transferred staff will be treated as before, protecting their terms and conditions, as TUPE shall apply. Further, the CoP seeks to ensure parity by way of a level playing field where 'new joiners' are treated. It prescribes that new joiners' employment terms should be on *"fair and reasonable terms and conditions which are, overall, no less favourable than those transferred employees"*. As previously noted in Chapter 3, pension provision before and after transfer should be "comparable".

5.3. Contracting-Out and TUPE

From 1979 onwards, the UK government introduced CCT in the public sector in order to increase efficiency and derive better value for money from service providers. Sceptical trade unionists believed that it was really an attempt to drive down wages and weaken employment rights in the public sector. In general employment law terms, contracting-out contributed to the disintegration of both traditional patterns of labour and business organisations themselves.

After nearly 20 years of legal wrangling before the ECJ on the scope of the TUPE Regulations, as discussed in Chapter 2, the UK government's established general guidance on contracting-out issued on the 11 March 1993 advised contractors to evade TUPE by widely and creatively utilising the economic, technical or organisational (ETO) defences, contained in Article 4 of the ARD and Regulation 8 of the TUPE Regulations 1981. In particular, Paragraph 9 of the UK government's guidance advised that within TUPE lies an opt-out criterion from the protection granted by the ARD. All of these ETO defences are justifiable reasons for reducing labour costs and the workforce generally, either before or after a business transfer, whether instigated by CCT or not. The promotion of the wide-usage of these defences displays the UK government's defiance against the *Rask* decision, already discussed in Chapter 2, which allowed employees subjected to contracting-out to be protected by the ARD (in the UK, TUPE).

It has been stated that avoidance of TUPE gives cost benefits. Many contractors continue to argue that if TUPE applies then, they would not be able to compete with either the Direct Service Organisations (DSO)/in-house provider (the in-house, existing service providers who executed the service prior to the contracting-out regime), or the current service provider (the competitor). This is an argument which the UK government preserved in its CCT policy and thus simultaneously, in its approach towards TUPE and the ARD. Hence, it could be argued that any business transfers under contracting-out could potentially be justified on ETO grounds. These ETO defences, therefore, could undermine the TUPE Regulations whilst increasing efficiency and competitiveness.

Since the Conservatives' 1992 Election Manifesto, which made specific reference to 'bringing the private-sector enterprise into the public services', CCT has been implemented in many areas of both central and local government activities. The 1980 and 1988 Local Government Acts, as well as the NHS & Community Care Act 1990, the Civil Service (Management Functions) Act 1992, the Criminal Justice & Public Order Act 1994 and the Deregulation & Contracting Out Act 1994, heralded the restructuring of the UK public sector. Contracting-out has involved restructuring in both blue and white collar services previously provided by local authorities, the health service and central government. Following a test run with building services under the Local Government Planning & Land Act 1980, the Local Government Act 1988 introduced CCT to refuse collection, cleaning, catering and leisure facilities as the next areas to be exposed to market forces.

A tendering process lies at the heart of all of these statutory schemes. They all commence with a service provider, such as a local authority or hospital, putting out a particular service to tender. The local authority/council or health authority, becomes known thereafter as the 'client side'. The tendering process begins with a 'Contract Specification', being drafted, followed by the publication and circulation of a notice of intention to tender in the press. Before the specification is concluded, some consideration should be afforded to staffing issues. The process continues with the tenderers replying to the advertisements by submitting a tender document, commonly referred to solely as a 'tender', within 37 days. A 'tender' has to be made in writing and be a signed statement making a bid and stating that the contractor, at this stage the 'tenderer' will supply services for a given price. Following the submission of the bids, an evaluation of the bids takes place which is followed by an awarding of the contract. There are usually 120 days between the awarding of the contract and its commencement. Thereafter, the contractor is referred to as the 'service provider'. The evaluation process considers various factors, such as the costs of awarding the work to an external contractor, redundancy payments, matters relating to the tenderer's financial standing, geographical factors, the contractor's local knowledge and the tender price. A maximum of 90 days is set for tender evaluation. These tender documents substantiate a draft contract giving details of the contractor/service provider's practices as an employer. These will include information on grievance and disciplinary procedures; staff training; standards of service; staff uniforms; health and safety at work policies; and details about the re-employment of existing staff. Once the invitation period to tender closes, the existing service provider, strongly influenced by what is already being provided by in-house providers, selects a contractor.

Throughout this tendering process, the council/health authority, the original client-side service provider is obliged to: publish a notice of tender in a local newspaper, eliciting applications to appear on a list of nominated contractors; issue a reasonable specification; send out invitations to tender; invite written bids from the direct service organisation (DSO)/in-house provider; ensure that fair competition between all bidders exists; and explain their decision in favour of a particular bidder. This transparent tendering process ensures that information is given to all parties concerned and thus, lowers the prospects of uncertainty and misunderstanding between the parties concerned, thereby reducing the risk of contractor failure. In any event, should such communication breakdown, then aggrieved tenderers can complain to the Office of Deputy Prime Minister (ODPM), whereupon the Minister could award the contract if it deems the client-side, original service provider to have acted out of its obligations, by issuing a Section 13 Order.

5.4. Ordinary Transfers versus Contracting-Out Transfers

Such an expansive statutory framework, rooted in competition and best value policy has affected TUPE. In practical terms, it emerges that two categories of transfer arise: ordinary or contracting-out. In order to distinguish the two categories, contracting-out (or contracting-in), prevails in three situations: an organisation contracts out a contract for goods or services for the first time (first generation); or the first contractor is replaced by a second, third, fourth, etc contractor (second generation); or, the client takes the contracted-out activities back in-house (contracting-in). All other situations are ordinary sales of businesses (hence ordinary business transfers). Note it is only under contracting scenarios that TUPE can frustrate the seller's and purchaser's commercial intentions. TUPE will not apply if the contract is won on a contracting-out basis by an in-house team because there is no change of employer.

Transfers back and forth between contractors can also pose problems under TUPE. For example, in the case of *MOD v Clutterbuck*[1], the EAT was asked to consider the situation where Mr Clutterbuck, who was originally employed by the MOD, was transferred to a private contractor and was then at a later date subsequently transferred back into employment with

[1] MOD v. Clutterbuck [2000] IDS Brief 662 EAT

the MOD. The question arose: which contract was transferred; i.e. was it the original contract under which he had been employed by the MOD, or the later contract under which he had been employed by the private contractor? The EAT determined that it was the latter contract, that is, the contract with the private contractor, which passed back to the MOD.

5.5.   Practical Issues on TUPE with Contracting-Out

Irrespective of whether the business transfer results from a contracting-out exercise or not, it is vital for the both the seller and purchaser to give full consideration to TUPE issues. In particular, the stages, processes and principles set out in Chapter 2 demonstrated how important the contractual issues are and this may be more important in the context of contracting-out transfers, since a major criticism of contracting-out has been that it establishes a multifarious tangle of contractual relationships rather than one single economic unit. Arguably, the creation of a network of separate contractor units allows for greater flexibility in the employment environment. Such presents the first practical problem for TUPE: who is the employer and who are the employees, in terms of contractual issues? Therefore, a due diligence exercise is very important in order to ascertain the rights and liabilities involved.

Within the context of contracting-out transfers, the final written agreement may include the sale of assets, both tangible and intangible (such as goodwill) and the transfer of employees. Consequently, such an agreement may either contract in or out the services. To that end, the parties should specify which it is for the sake of clarity in terms of the application of TUPE. Can TUPE ever be evaded? TUPE is not there to be evaded and the courts must prevent this from occurring. Regulation 12 of the TUPE Regulations 1981 provided that *'Any provision of any agreement…shall be void in so far as it purports to exclude or limit the operation of Regulation 5, 8 or 10'*. This is now replicated under Regulation 17 of the TUPE Regulations 2006.

However, such wording can be avoided under a compromise agreement regulated by section 203 of the ERA 1996 (the latter agreement being binding and valid); and, the transferee may refuse to take on the staff subject to transfer. The latter prevails as the weakest of the two options and likely to be questionable before the courts following the *ECM v. Cox*, already discussed.

It emerges that the test as to whether TUPE applies in contracting-out situations is now recognised to be no different from the test as to whether TUPE applies in the context of an ordinary business transfer, since you need to identify a stable economic entity (i.e. identify the assets, be they production or employees). If a significant proportion transfers, then TUPE automatically applies. Whether TUPE applies or not is the question of fact in each case, but the starting point for contracting-out should be to assume that TUPE applies.

More practical problems arise in second generation contracting-out. This is simply because the first generation (original) client and contractor will have set the standard having negotiated a contract (or service level agreement) with relevant warranties and indemnities. Clearly, there is limited scope for the second round contractor, since there is no contract between it and the outgoing contractor and a limited scope for obtaining information exists. The remedy available for this is to stipulate in the first contract that the first contractor must indemnify subsequent contractors for the first contractor's acts or omissions, as well as providing information and documentation concerning its employees at the end of the contract period.

To ease practical problems in the public sector the UK Government has issued a 'Statement of Practice' setting out the principles that should apply to the public sector. This specifies that all contracting-out should apply TUPE, including all second generation exercises and even where in limited circumstances TUPE may not apply, the TUPE principles should be adhered to. However, this Statement only applies to the transfer of staff from the public sector to the private or voluntary sectors.

Pensions, as in ordinary transfer cases, are a further contentious issue in contracting-out. The practical problem here is the difference in pension provision between the public and private sectors. The guiding principle should be that the new employer must offer those staff affected membership of a 'broadly comparable' pension scheme, as previously discussed in Chapter 3.

Another practical problem, presented by TUPE to contracting-out situations, is that public sector trade union recognition is more common that in the private sector. A private sector contractor may then find itself dealing with a collective environment with which it is unfamiliar with. Apart from the obvious solution of de-recognition, in light of the ERA such a solution may be difficult given the procedural mechanics involved. A related issue is that of consultation; where no previous experience of unions/employee representatives exists, then the need to create consultation arrangements is necessary as previously discussed.

The final practical problem is that of equal pay and is particularly pertinent to the public sector. Notably, the Equal Pay Act 1970 provides that the claimant must show a comparator, broadly undertaking the same or like work, employed on common terms and conditions. Whilst job evaluation schemes are common in the public sector, North Yorkshire County Council paid out £4 million to employees having been dismissed and re-employed on a lower rate of pay in order to reduce costs. The House of Lords in *Ratcliffe v. North Yorkshire County Council*,[2] held that the need to cut costs was not a material factor and therefore not a defence.

5.6. SPC, TUPE and the Law

English law's recognition of the existence of contracting-out, was first noted in the *Rastill*[3] decision. Since then, three important decisions of the ECJ with regard to contracting-out, notably *Rask*, *Schmidt* and *Rygaard*, have arisen. At a domestic level, many attempts have been made to evade the obligations under TUPE, especially by those in pursuit of contracting-out, or a contractor's primary aim being to seek out lower unit labour costs. This objective has confronted the TUPE's primary aim to protect employees' rights subjected to transfers. The ECJ has issued a series of determinations making it clear that it is prepared to uphold the ARD's principles, for example in the *Rask* and *Schmidt* decisions, previously discussed, where the ECJ held that such contracting out was protected under the Directive and that the ARD explicitly applied to contracting-out.

In the UK, the *Dines* case introduced at the outset of this text, highlights that contracting-out will not be allowed to impede the worker's protection afforded by TUPE. The central well-rehearsed question in this case was whether there was an identifiable economic entity and whether it had been disposed of as a going concern? In order to answer this question, applying the ECJ's rulings in the *Spijkers* and *Rask* cases, already discussed in Chapter 2, and the UK Court of Appeal's judgment in *Dines*, enables the enquirer to establish whether there is a business transfer by deciding whether the business retains its identity or not.

The decision of the House of Lords in *North Yorkshire County Council v. Ratcliffe*[4], involving the contracting-out of provision of school meals under the Local Government Act 1988, recognised that CCT threatened the status quo in working conditions and employment protection. The complexity surrounding this misconceived equal pay claim arose with regard to

---

[2] Ratcliffe v. North Yorks. CC [1995] IRLR 439 HL

[3] Rastill v. Automatic Refreshment Service Ltd [1978] ICR 289

[4] North Yorkshire County Council v. Ratcliffe [1995] ICR 833, 839

whether an employer can rely upon external market forces as a defence for discriminatory changes in the rates of pay. The Court of Appeal had earlier concluded that the market forces defence was a reasonable justification, that the operation of contracting-out does amount to a transfer, and that the UK's TUPE Regulations were in breach of the EU's directive on transfers. The ET at an earlier hearing had misdirected itself in holding that when there is a change of contractors, there is a cessation of the business and that business transfers may take place in two or more phases. The House of Lords overturning the Court of Appeal's ruling dismissed the economic defence, presented as a genuine material factor, permissible in Equal Pay cases in certain circumstances, similar to the ETO for business transfers.

Lord Slynn's leading speech revitalised hope anew for those subject to contracting-out transfers by placing economics second to employee's rights. Following *Dines* and *Schmidt*, an acceptance of CCT under the scope of the ARD could now provoke a wider-usage of the ETO defences, particularly since CCT is an example of market forces at work. And so, it can be intimated that a CCT transfer inherently gives rise to an automatic ETO defence. We will return to this growing important issue in the next section of this chapter.

Nevertheless, other decisions of the UK courts before *Dines* have shown other procedural ways and means of complaining about dismissals in connection with transfers. Two important domestic decisions, *Kenny*[5] and *Porter*[6], demonstrate that action against dismissal by way of business transfer can alternatively be initiated in the High Court. For example, in *Kenny*, a case involving lecturers at Her Majesty's Youth Custody Centre (HMYCC) Thorn Cross who underwent a CCT exercise and a subsequent business transfer, the High Court held that a legal business transfer had occurred since the business transferred had retained its identity.

In the *Porter* case, the plaintiffs seeking a declaration were employees of Trent Regional Health Authority, employed as consultant paediatricians, at Kesteven General Hospital. Following the conviction of Beverly Allitt, a former paediatric nurse at Kesteven General Hospital, after an enquiry into the deaths of babies, the Trent Regional Health Authority terminated their arrangements with the Kesteven Hospital and entered into a contract with another NHS Trust for the provision of paediatric provisions. The 'new'

---

[5] Kenny v. South Manchester College [1993] IRLR 265 QBD

[6] Porter & Nanayakkara v. Queen's Medical Centre (Nottingham University Hospital) [1993] IRLR 486 QBD

contractor created four consultant paediatric posts to service the contract. However, the Regional Health Authority asked the NHS Trust Contractor to re-engage all staff, including the plaintiffs. They did warn Porter and others that it might lead to the posts becoming redundant. On 25 March the Regional Health Authority sent Porter *et al* formal notices of their redundancy. On 30 April, Porter and others were interviewed for the vacant posts, but were unsuccessful.

Subsequently, Porter sought a declaration that their contracts of employment took effect as originally made with the defendants rather than the Regional Health Authority. Porter contended that the reorganisation fell within the ARD, since an undertaking had been transferred. Furthermore, the Regional Health Authority disputed that there had been any termination of the contract and that the ARD did not apply in the instant case. They conceded that TUPE did not give full effect to the ARD which was directly enforceable against a public body, such as an NHS Trust. The High Court held that Order 14A was appropriate where the plaintiffs, Porter *et al*, could establish facts which showed that the conclusion must be that there was a business transfer. The court's reasoning being that a 'relevant' business transfer, despite section 4(3) of the NHS & Community Care Act 1990 which does not deprive an NHS contract of its legal effect, was effected. A business transfer being established under Article 1(1) of the ARD and following the ECJ's pronouncement in *Redmond*, where a change in the provider of such services brought about a business transfer as the responsibilities of the Regional Health Authority remained unchanged.

It remains a growing anxiety amongst lawyers that the legal pronouncements on contracting-out could merely be the tip of the iceberg, since a further problem may be encountered in the not too distant future. For instance, the EAT upheld that contracting-in amounted to a transfer in the *Brintel Helicopters*[7] case. 'Contracting-in' is a term used to define a situation where the "client" resumes the service provision which they undertook before the first contracting out exercise took place. The facts of the Brintel Helicopters case are that the Isles of Scilly Council owned and managed St Mary's Airport until 1986, when they decided to seek tenders for the management contract. Subsequently, Brintel Helicopters became the service provider. The contract was terminated on 1 January 1993 and all employees concerned were made redundant. After the event they were re-

---

[7] Council of the Isles of Scilly v. Brintel Helicopters Ltd [1995] IRLR 6 EAT

employed by the Council on less favourable terms and conditions. An ET upheld the employees' complaints, since there was a sufficient 'economic' entity. The council appealed to the EAT on the ground that there was no business transfer. Adopting a purposive approach and the Court of Appeal's guidance in the *Dines* decision, the EAT dismissed the appeal having established a transferable 'economic entity', by rejecting the contention that a 'labour only business' prevented a business transfer from occurring.

In terms of further clarification, the Scottish EAT in the *Kelman*[8] case applied *Dines*, the EAT's decision in *Brintel* and the ECJ's ruling in *Schmidt*, to hold that a business transfer had occurred since the identity of the undertaking had survived the business transfer. *Kelman* was another case involving a CCT exercise under the Local Government Act 1988. Following the tendering exercise, Grampian Direct Services Organisation (GDSO) took charge for the provision of school cleaning in from 1 January 1989. Between 1989 and 1992, the cleaners experienced no change. The GDSO was not as successful in the re-tendering exercise in 1992, obtaining only four out of the five contracts. Consequently, the fifth area was awarded to Care Contract Services Ltd and Phyliss Kelman and others were made redundant. She had been a supervisor earning £4.04 an hour but was offered only £3.38 an hour by the 'new' service provider. Mrs Kelman complained to an ET. The ET found no 'TUPE transfer' had occurred, although the EAT with the benefit of the ECJ's recent ruling in *Schmidt* found to the contrary and upheld Mrs Kelman's claim. This decision, to some degree, clarifies the law, which is much welcomed.

Returning briefly to the issue of contracting-out and discrimination, the EAT in the *DJM International Ltd. v. Nicholas*[9] case held that liability for sex discrimination could be transferred following a business transfer. Despite the fact that the alleged act of discrimination concerned took place before the business transfer under a previous contract of employment, once the business is transferred the liability for that discrimination also becomes transferable. In the words of the President of the EAT, Mummery J.:
"...a liability may be incurred by an employer to an employee and that subsequent change in the contractual relationship between the employer and employee does not prevent that liability from transferring to the transferee of the undertaking".

---

[8] Kelman v. Care Contract Services Ltd & Grampian Regional Council [1995] ICR 260 EAT

[9] DJM International Ltd v. Nicholas [1996] IRLR 76 EAT

The House of Lords' decision in the *Ratcliffe* case goes some way to confirm the potential of such a claim by the Equality and Human Rights Commission (EHRC)[10]. This is to be discussed later. Similarly, the case of the former Cleveland County Council dinner ladies' claim for sex discrimination, when they were contracted-out and lost their holiday pay during vacations whilst the male workers kept theirs, was deemed to be sex discrimination and resulted in out of tribunal awards of compensation.

Following these decisions, practitioners now find it increasingly difficult to advise where contracting-out, or any change of service provider, will not be covered by TUPE. In particular, the *Betts* decision poses a future problem, when contracting-out comes to an end and the previous provider resumes control. Ostensibly, the growing UK common law surrounding the ARD and TUPE alike following ECJ rulings has either assisted in clarifying the law, or mystifying the parties involved. The latter being due to incremental nature of the ETO defences being used by contractors' lawyers. Clearly, the 1977 ARD and the TUPE Regulations 1981 have been the legal instruments which have been solely held together by ECJ's rulings and clarifications delivered by both the EAT and Court of Appeal. Much of the recent uncertainty surrounding business transfers has been presented by the UK's contracting-out policy.

5.7.   The 'ETO' Defences and contracting

From the preceding chapters, one could rightly have drawn the conclusion that TUPE is a one-sided piece of legislation solely in favour of protecting workers' rights. As HR and legal practitioners alike know, that is not so since the ETO defences preserve the EU Commission's original intentions of encouraging market harmonisation. Article 4(1) of the ARD expressly limits its application on dismissals subject to ETO reasons which the employer can give.

The ETO defences have attracted little attention from the ECJ and the EU Commission. Following their Lordships' deliberations in the *Ratcliffe* case, discussed above, much of the debate surrounding business transfers has now moved towards the applicability of the ETO defences. Regulation 8 of the TUPE Regulations 1981 provided three defences. These defences were derived from Article 4 of the ARD. Though, Regulation 8(1) provided that:
"where either before or after a relevant transfer, any employee of the transferor or transferee is dismissed, that employee shall be treated...as unfairly dismissed if the transfer or a reason connected with it is the reason or principal reason for his

---

[10] Which replaced the EOC with the implementation of the Equality Act 2010

dismissal". This automatic unfairness rule is linked to the 'escape route' provided for under regulation 8(2) which stated that: "where an economic, technical or organisational reason entailing changes in the workforce of either the transferor or the transferee before or after a relevant transfer, is the reason or principal reason for dismissing the employee".

The EU passivity on these ETO defences might be explained by the opinions of Advocate-Generals in two leading ECJ rulings. For instance, Advocate-General Darmon in *Bork*[11] suggested that the ETO defences were restricted where: *"...the undertaking's resumption of business was envisaged".* This declaration has led the ECJ to believe that the applicability of the ETO defences is narrow and most certainly inapplicable should the business continue post-transfer. Following this advice, the ECJ held that Article 4(1) of the ARD shall not in itself constitute grounds for dismissal and that the employees transferred were to be treated as still employed, albeit now by the transferee. Relying upon Darmon's comments in *Bork*, Advocate-General Van Gerven, some three years later, in *D'Urso*, restated more vociferously that the ARD:

"expressly prohibits dismissals when they are the result of the transfer of the undertaking. Only dismissals which would have been made in any case, for instance if the decision was taken before there was any question of transferring the undertaking, fall within the exclusion. Article 4 cannot therefore be relied upon as a support for an argument for dismissing some of the employees because the undertaking has been transferred".

Van Gerven therefore concludes that the ETO defences cannot be relied upon as a justification for dismissals. However, the ECJ in *D'Urso* whilst generally approving of the Advocate-General's advice, stated that although Article 4(1) of the ARD forbade: *"...the use of the transfer itself as a reason for dismissal...on the other hand, the Directive shall not stand in the way of dismissals which may take place for economic, technical or organisational reasons".* The contradictory nature of the ECJ's approach to the ETO defences perhaps explains the ECJ's passivity on these ETO defences. Nevertheless, the debate surrounding the ARD, having moved on from the scope of the ARD, now lies in answering the question of whether there is an ETO reason. The central issue here is what constitutes an 'ETO' defence? Although, it is now clear when it should apply, the question of when they are appropriate not only depends upon the fact, but also on their definition. The original and the amended ARDs, as well as the 1981 and 2006 TUPE

---

[11] Bork (P) International A/S v. Foreningen af Arbejdsledere i Danmark [1989] IRLR 41 ECJ

Regulations all fail to define them and more recently, EU legislators sought not to define them in their proposed revision of the ARD. The ECJ has also yet to rule on this specific issue up to now has also not ruled on this issue.

Economic

The UK government sought to define these terms in its guidance issued in March 1993, when William Waldegrave MP, then the Chancellor of the Duchy of Lancaster, defined 'economic' to mean: *"where a demand for an employer's output has fallen that profitability could not be sustained"*; 'technical' referred to the usage of: *"new technology and the employees did not have the necessary skills"*; and he described 'organisational' as a situation which arises: *"where a new employer operates at a different location and it is not practical to relocate"*. Overall, this exercise recognised that the UK courts had tended towards a narrow interpretation of such reasons, but that in such cases dismissal might be fair provided the employer had acted reasonably to allow an exclusion.

Previous cases have considered what is meant by the term 'economic'. For instance, in the Scottish EAT, the case of *Meikle v. McPhail (Charlston Arms)*[12] held that the term connoted a commercial objective. This case concerned the transfer of a pub which was in the opinion of the new employer and publican, overstaffed. Ostensibly, the new owner, the transferee, soon realised that unless he made a staff reduction, the business could not be run profitably. This argument lends support to the view that purpose of the ETO defences is to remove the actual economic burdens from new employers when subjected to business transfers, by sanctioning so-called 'economic dismissal'.

Technical

No cases at present have addressed what is meant by the term 'technical', although it is commonly assumed that this covers situations where an employee is dismissed because s/he does not have the necessary technical know-how or experience for the job which has changed for technological reasons, for example, requiring the use of new equipment. This might include in a contracting-out context, the usage of 'wheelie bins' replacing old static waste or refuse bins, or the usage of larger vehicles or different machinery.

---

[12] Meikle v. McPhail (Charleston Arms) [1983] IRLR 351 Scot. EAT

Organisation

The High Court has summarily adjudicated on what is meant by 'organisational' in the *Porter* case, as mentioned above. In the context of the ETO defence, the defendants contended that the redundancy notices issued to the appellants were issued for organisational reasons. This case an example of where a public body decided to terminate its arrangement with one person and replace it with an arrangement with another having similar aims and as part of this process a business reorganisation was also incurred resulting in the dismissal of some employees. The defendants argued that it was for this reason that the plaintiffs were dismissed. The Court stated, per Sir Godfray Le Quesne, that:

"I have no doubt that this amounted to a reorganisation of the services. It cannot be said that the reorganisation did not entail changes in the workforce because the defendants should have appointed the plaintiffs to the positions for which they had applied. The relevant change in the workforce, as I have said was in my view the termination of the existing contracts of the Plaintiffs. That is the change which was entailed by the organisational reasons".

The peculiar outcome of the *Porter* case throws the effectiveness of the legislation open to question, particularly when, despite the ARD's declared aim, the Directive did also provide for ETO justifications. The fact remains that although TUPE might apply, the ETO defences could rescue an employer from any liability. It may be that the long-term effect of the *Porter* decision will be that the ETO defences can now be used by employers who undertake contracting-out business transfers. This is a situation which raises widespread concern amongst UK trade unions. Following *Porter*, applying Article 4(1) of the ARD, providing that a business transfer: *"shall not of itself constitute grounds for dismissal by the transferor or the transferee"*, to CCT business transfers means that the ETO justifications can indirectly prevail and any notices of termination served upon employees pre or post-transfer will not automatically be invalid at common law. Under the ARD, Article 3 provides for these rights to be carried post-transfer. Since there had been a valid termination, in *Porter* the plaintiffs were redundant. The court in dismissing the application addressed the central questions of whether there was a business transfer and whether this had been the result of a legal business transfer. Essentially, the High Court in *Porter* decided that the Regional Health Authority's decision to transfer its contract for the provision of paediatric services from one of its hospitals to an NHS Trust was a business transfer covered by the ARD. Thus, the contracts of employment of two consultants who had worked under the old contract would be transferred to the Trust. The ARD did not prevent the termination of the consultants' contracts by allowing the Trust to have an unrestricted choice as to who to appoint to the consultants' posts in the new service on the grounds of an organisational defence.

The decision of the EAT in the case of *BSG Property Services v Tuck and others*[13] has at last placed the ETO defences on the legal agenda. For a while now many HR and legal practitioners have awaited the debate surrounding business transfers to move on from the now well-trod path of how to identify 'a relevant transfer' and whether contracting-out is within the scope of the ARD, to what is meant in both the Directive and the TUPE Regulations by the term 'ETO'. The facts of this case concern the Mid-Bedfordshire District Council Housing Maintenance Direct Service Organisation (DSO), which employed a team of 14 jobbers, including Mr Tuck, a carpenter and other joiners, plumbers and bricklayers until the DSO decided to terminate their contracts with the Council on 12 February 1993. This litigation arose because three months later, in May 1993, the Council following a re-tendering exercise contracted with BSG Property Services to provide the housing maintenance formerly operated by the DSO. It was agreed between the Council and BSG that the work carried out by Tuck and others was to be undertaken by self-employed tradesmen. Both the Council and the 'new' contractor believed that TUPE did not apply, as they concluded that there was no transfer of an undertaking. Subsequently, the employment of Tuck and the other workers by Tuck and the DSO was terminated on the grounds of redundancy. Tuck and the other workers decided to claim unfair dismissal.

An ET found that a relevant transfer had occurred and that the dismissals were connected with the transfer, although the tribunal also took the view that they were not unfairly dismissed. The ET also held that redundancy was the reason for the dismissal and that BSG did not engage any employees was due to economic or organisational reasons within Regulation 8(2)(b). The employees' claims therefore failed. On appeal, Tuck and others appealed against the finding of an ETO defence and BSG appealed on the grounds that the tribunal had established that a transfer had occurred.

The EAT held that the tribunal had not erred in holding that a transfer had taken place. Considering all the facts, the EAT established that the activities concerned constituted an 'undertaking' capable of being transferred. Applying the Court of Appeal's approach in *Dines* and the ECJ's ruling in

---

[13] BSG Property Services v. Tuck [1996] IRLR 134 EAT

the *Rygaard* case, Mummery J. held that a 'stable economic entity' had been transferred. Considering all the relevant case law, the EAT reiterated that where an employee is dismissed by the transferor, even if the contract expires after the transfer, it is the transferor who dismisses. Accordingly the relevant reason for the dismissal is determined by the transferor, the council, despite liability for the dismissal connected with the transfer being passed to the transferee, BSG. It followed therefore that the Council's reason for the dismissals was the relevant reason. Relying upon the former relevant statutory provisions, sections 53, 54(1) and 55(2) of the then EPCA 1978, and the principle enunciated in *Devis & Sons v. Atkins*[14], the reason given by the Council on the effective date of termination and in writing thereafter was the reason for the dismissal.

On the facts, the EAT agreed that the tribunal had incorrectly found the Council had an ETO defence for the dismissals. The EAT ruled that because the Council and BSG did not believe that TUPE applied then no ETO defences could arise in the instant case. Recognition and admission of the existence of a TUPE transfer, therefore, becomes a precondition for the ETO defences. In addition, BSG in not believing that TUPE applied did not consider themselves to be the transferee at all, although, under Regulation 5, they were subject to all the liabilities of the Council on connection with the contracts of employment. Had no transfer occurred, then the Council would have remained liable. As for the transferee, although it did not dismiss, but as a result of a transfer became liable for the dismissal, then it was bound by the Council's reason which did not give rise to an ETO defence. The interesting point which the EAT raises in its decision in this case is that no ETO reason can be relied upon unless TUPE applies. In Mummery J.'s words: *"They did not believe that they had to have such a reason, because they did not believe that the 1981 Regulations applied"*. It could not be any clearer that a belief that TUPE does not apply means that no ETO defence can be considered or otherwise arise as a reason for the transfer, should one be established. In addition, the EAT confirmed that a transferee is bound by the transferor's reasons. It therefore remains clear law that Regulation 8's automatic unfairness rule applies to dismissals whether they are effected before or after the date of the business transfer, without any specific limitation in time.

Essentially, the EAT ruling produces a three stage test when applicants or appellants alike seek to rely upon the ETO defences:

---

[14] Devis & Sons v. Atkins [1977] IRLR 314 HL

1. it must be established that an ETO reason was connected with the business transfer;
2. an onus is on the employer to show that the principal reason falls within the scope of Regulation 8 which entails changes in the workforce; and
3. the reasonableness of the decision must be assessed in all the circumstances.

This threefold test requires a link between a dismissal and a business transfer. A test which confirms the EAT's ruling is *Wheeler*, a case involving the transfer of a business where the prospective purchaser insisted upon the dismissal of all the existing staff. The EAT concluded that an 'economic' reason for dismissal to fall within Regulation 8(2) of the TUPE Regulations 1981 must be one which relates to the conduct of the business. The EAT in the *Wheeler* case provides some restraint on recalcitrant employers who undertake transfers and attempt to hide behind the ETO defences. It was held that in order to shield a business by an ETO reason for the transfer, the conduct of the business must give rise to such a defence.

Evidently, the ETO defences raise more specific questions in respect of contracting-out. That being so, does any contracting-out exercise inherently have an economic defence? If so, that might be met with further confusion amongst the judges, as already seen in non-contracting out cases. For example, in *Trafford v. Sharpe*[15], involving redundancies post-transfer, the EAT considered an ETO defence.

Adopting a purposive approach towards the construction of Regulation 8, Mummery J. stated that:
"The rights of workers must be safeguarded 'so far as possible'. It is not always possible to safeguard the rights of workers. As is recognised...the rights of workers not to be dismissed on the transfer of an undertaking must not stand in the way of dismissals which take place for economic reasons entailing changes in the workforce. In such cases the rights of workers may be outweighed by the economic reasons".

The question arises as to whose economic reason was Mummery J. referring? This decision presents ambiguity, in so far as it reinforced usage of the ETO defences and asserted that the ARD no longer safeguards the employee first and foremost. Instead the primary objective of the ARD is subject to a weighing up of the employer's economic situation against the

---

[15] Trafford v. Sharpe [1994] IRLR 325 EAT

employee's livelihood. Such a decision sends out a clear message to employers to evade the legislation.

This lies in stark contrast to the House of Lords' decision in the *Ratcliffe* case, previously discussed. Applying the House of Lord's ruling to business transfers, rather than the Equal Pay Act which the case concerned, such an evasion of the Regulations was exactly what the ARD was seeking to prevent. As we are already aware, the ARD exists in an attempt to safeguard the rights of employees. Lord Slynn, giving the leading judgment, rejected the economic reason forwarded by the Council for the pay decreases incurred by their former employees post-transfer. In Lord Slynn's words: *"Though conscious of the difficult problem facing the employers in seeking to compete with a rival,...that...was the very kind of discrimination in relation to pay which the Act sought to remove"*. Whilst these cases concern solely the 'economic' aspect of the ETO defences, Scott J. in the *Wheeler* case affirmed that: *"...the adjective, 'economic', must be construed ejusdem generis with the adjective 'technical' and 'organisational'"*.

Applying such deliberations to contracting-out cases, the ETO defences might not be easily utilised. As already argued the *Ratcliffe* case could have been successfully framed under the ARD, though the same question about economic and social rights would have arisen. As it did regarding equal pay in *Ratcliffe*, it will do so where CCT business transfers as outsourcing exercises are economically motivated. Again, Scott J.'s guidance in *Wheeler* adds some further light onto the issue, when the EAT suggested that any reasons for dismissals should be *"genuinely economic, technical or organisational"*. The term 'genuinely' will either permit the extension of these defences or restrict them.

It would appear that the *Tuck* case pushes the future debate surrounding business transfers into a discussion about the applicability and substance of the much-quoted and until now, little used, ETO defences. This decision of the EAT presents another problem for those concerned with business transfers. Will contractors now accept that TUPE applies and agree on an ETO reason before transfers take place? The central question remains unanswered; how will the courts in the UK or the ECJ interpret these ETO defences? Perhaps, upon reflection, the former President of the EAT's words might never have been so apt, at least for the present if not in the future:

"The TUPE Regulations continue to yield fresh problems particularly in the area of the contracting out of services by public authorities"

The wider definition of business transfer adopted by *Rask* shows that TUPE does apply to contracting out. Successive restatements of this position clearly enunciated in *Schmidt*, *Dines* and *Wren* have major implications for the UK government's contracting-out policy. In essence, employees affected by contracting-out now retain their continuity of employment. Local and Health Authorities *et al*, the previous providers, are now liable for redundancy payments; new contractors will be expected to continue contractually agreed salaries and terms; and most significantly, any dismissal connected with contracting-out transfers will be deemed automatically unfair, unless the ETO defences apply. As a result, private contractors will no longer be able to submit successful tender bids on the basis of lower labour costs, since the ARD ensures that terms and conditions of employment are unchanged, except in respect of those pension rights which are prevented from transferring as a result of the pensions exclusion discussed in Chapter 3. Thus, the usual rationale for contracting out centred on reducing public expenditure could be fatally undermined. Contractors are now less likely to be willing to make bids without an indemnity for dismissal costs and redundancies from the previous provider.

As has already been identified, differing judicial attitudes emerge amidst the respective approaches adopted by the UK and EU judges. The EU judges have adopted a 'purposive' interpretation which has reluctantly been adopted by the UK judiciary. Previously, the UK judges' approach can be traced back to their support of the widely-used 'managerial prerogative', meaning that the reason of 'business efficacy' is used to justify employers' policies. Case law reveals a revival in the importance of economics, and this coupled with an anticipated wider-usage of the ETO defences (as implied in the *Dines* and *Tuck* decisions) suggests that the British tradition, enshrined in laissez-faire and the freedom of contract, could prevail. However, the possibility should not be dismissed that as UK judges acquaint themselves (like both their EU and US counterparts) with some basic economic thinking following the *Ratcliffe* case, the EU teleological approach might even yet prevail in UK judicial deliberations. Although only 14 cases, since 1983 to date, have considered the importance of ETO defences, an upturn in this trend is likely following *Dines*. The potential economic aspects of the ETO defences could therefore have been widened, particularly with regard to contracting-out business transfers, which are undeniably a result of economic circumstances. The main reason why an increase in the usage of these defences is anticipated is the fact that the terms themselves, 'economic', 'technical' or 'organisational' are not defined. Like the SOSR justification, the ETO defences remain sufficiently vague, so as to allow the users of these defences to mould them as their discretion and circumstances permit. It also allows the courts and tribunals discretion to decide what is reasonable when utilised.

The EAT's latest guidance on the usage of the 'some other substantial reason' (SOSR) justification requires a focus upon the extent to which the dismissals or redundancies are due to the reason given.

This guidance does very little to prevent the usage of the ETO defences when confronted with a contracting-out business transfer. The EAT instituting its new test for SOSR, found that even where a sound 'business reason' is given, the balance between the disadvantages of the new terms to the employees and the advantages to the employers must be undertaken. In light of the last test, one might argue that the ETO defences might even be restricted in a contracting-out context, even where the employer can justify the less favourable terms as a consequence of the mechanics of contracting-out. Where the disadvantages to the employee are worsened to the employer's advantage an ETO defence might even then be rejected as unreasonable.

The *Wheeler v. Patel* case determined that to be an economic reason within the ETO defences, it must relate to the conduct of the business and not the sale of the business. However, in *Whitehouse v. Blatchford*[16], the EAT held that where the grant of a contract to the transferee was made conditional upon a reduction in the workforce then a dismissal in order to obtain a contract was distinct from a dismissal to secure a business transfer. The transfer was therefore merely the event for the dismissal and not the cause. Hence ETO applied. Moreover, a dismissal can be for ETO reasons even if the dismissal would not have been made but for the business transfer, as was the case in *Trafford v. Sharpe*[17] and *Warner v. Adnet*[18]. Yet in *Kerry Foods v. Creber*, the EAT decided that if the business transfer is the effective reason for the dismissal then the ETO defences should not apply. However, if the transfer was a reason for the dismissal, then the dismissal itself would not be automatically unfair. It is suggested that readers should be wary of the *Kerry Foods* decision given that it is arguably inconsistent with TUPE and, therefore, potentially incorrect. More recently, the EAT in *Meter*

---

[16] Whitehouse v. Blatchford [1999] IRLR 49 EAT

[17] Trafford v. Sharpe [1994] IRLR 325 EAT

[18] Warner v. Adnet Ltd [1998] IRLR 394 EAT

U Ltd v. Ackroyd & Others[19], Slade J held that 'workforce' under Regulation 7(2) of TUPE 2006 did not include corporate franchisees, applying *Delabole*. Furthermore, Slade J held that without any diminution in the workforce, no ETO reasons arose.

As already mentioned, the fact that the primary legislation is committed to safeguarding employees' rights, yet simultaneously provides employers with defences, defies logic, since the ETO defences, when reasonably deployed, can defeat the legislation's aim. This somewhat inconsistent approach is the consequence of an EU compromise to assist employees, whilst remaining 'fair' to employers. However, the Court of Appeal in *Spaceright Europe Ltd v. Baillavoine*[20] clarified that a dismissal could be for a 'reason connected with the transfer' within Regulation 7(1) TUPE, even if there was no particular transfer in existence or in contemplation at the time of the dismissal.

5.8.   Recent developments on SPC

Since the enactment of the 2006 TUPE Regulations much of the early case law has sought (as seen in Chapter 4 on Insolvency) to dis-apply TUPE. Alternatively, fragmentation, post-transfer, has predominantly prevailed as an issue. Notably, the decisions in *Kimberley Group Housing Ltd v. Hambley*[21] and *Clearsprings Management Ltd v. Ankers, EAT*[22], in addition to determining how to apportion liabilities, confirmed that the approach where the services were so fragmented that a relevant transfer of undertakings from the original provider to the new provider could not be said to have occurred, as well as determining how to apportion liabilities, led to the conclusion that TUPE did not apply in such circumstances.

However, the EAT (HHJ Clark, presiding) in *Enterprise Management Services Ltd v. Connect-up Ltd*[23] restated the approach to be taken when evaluating whether a service provision change had taken place under Regulation 3(10(b) TUPE 2006, endorsing *Metropolitan Resources Ltd v. Churchill*[24].

---

[19] Meter U v Ackroyd & Others UKEAT/0206/11/CEA

[20] Spaceright Europe Ltd v. Baillavoine [2011] EWCA Civ 1565

[21] Kimberley Group Housing Ltd v. Hambley [2008] ICR 1030

[22] Clearsprings Management Ltd v. Ankers [2009], EAT

[23] Enterprise Management Services Ltd v. Connect-Up Ltd [2012] IRLR 190

[24] Metropolitan Resources Ltd v. Churchill [2009] IRLR 700

Further, in *Hunter v. McCarrick*[25] Slade J in the EAT clarified that Regulation 3(1)(b)(ii) TUPE 2006 provides that a service provision change (SPC) arises where activities cease to be carried out on a client's behalf and are instead carried out by a subsequent contractor on the client's behalf. Such an established formula being applied to this new concept, permitted the EAT to extol that such had to be read as meaning 'the same client'. Consequently, for there to be an SPC the activities must be carried out by different providers, both before and after the transfer, but for the same client.

It is worth reiterating the statutory provisions under scrutiny: Regulation 3 of the Transfer of Undertakings (Protection of Employment) Regulations 2006 (TUPE) provides:

"(1) These Regulations apply to —
(a)...
(b) a service provision change; that is, a situation in which —

> (i) *activities cease to be carried out by a person ("a client") on his own behalf and are carried out instead by another person on the client's behalf ("a contractor");*

> (ii) *activities cease to be carried out by a contractor on a client's behalf (whether or not those activities had previously been carried out by the client on its own behalf) and are carried out instead by another person ("a subsequent contractor") on the client's behalf; or*

> (iii) *activities cease to be carried out by a contractor or a subsequent contractor on a client's behalf (whether or not those activities had previously been carried out by the client on its own behalf) and are carried out instead by the client on his own behalf,and in which the conditions set out in paragraph (3) are satisfied."*

In *Metropolitan v Churchill Dulwich Ltd [2009] ICR 1380* the EAT held that:

"... The tribunal needs to ask itself whether the activities carried on by the alleged transferee are fundamentally or essentially the same as those carried out by the alleged transferor."

Minor or trivial differences in the "pre" and "post" activities were to be disregarded. Further, an SPC requires for there to be *"an organised grouping of employees"*. Applying *Metropolitan Resources Ltd v Churchill Dulwich Ltd* it is plainly an issue of what was or was not an activity as a matter of fact. The same approach was taken by the EAT in *Enterprise Management Services*

---

[25] Hunter v. McCarrick [2012], EAT

Ltd v. Connect-Up Ltd [2012] IRLR 190. The question is essentially a question of fact and degree.

The wording of TUPE looks to activities, *"that cease to be carried out by a client on his own behalf"*. The client is one and the same person as that expression is used throughout Regulation 3 (as approved by the Court of Appeal in *McCarrick v Hunter* [2012] EWCA Civ 1399). Accordingly, the Court of Appeal reiterates that we need to identify one "client".

For any SPC under TUPE, it is a requirement that:
"...the client intends that the activities will, following the service provision change, be carried out by the transferee other than in connection with a single specific event or task of short term duration..."

However, the issue is not whether the services would operate only in connection with a single specific event or a task of short term duration, but whether that was the intention of the client.

Dismissals for "an economic, technical or organisational reason" (ETO) under TUPE are potentially fair. In *The Manchester College v Hazel & Anor* the EAT had to consider whether dismissals for refusing to accept revised terms and conditions six months after a TUPE transfer, were ETO dismissals and whether orders for re-engagement were correctly made.

The next question is whether the dismissals were saved by ETO reasons under TUPE (i.e. an economic, technical or organisational reason entailing changes in the workforce).

Focussing on the words "entailing changes in the workforce", the issue is whether there had been a change in the workforce numbers (given that there were no changes in its functions). In *Meter U Ltd v Ackroyd* whilst the EAT considered that there is not a closed category of "changes in the workforce", it had yet to see any practical examples other than changes in numbers or functions. It was clear in that case that once the claimants were told that they were not at risk of redundancy and the redundancy process had ended, what was next on the agenda was harmonisation of conditions.

However, new terms are not a change in the workforce and so the ET majority was correct in its construction of TUPE. That meant the dismissals were automatically unfair.

In terms of the single specific event, the EAT in *Swanbridge v. Butler & Others* (Slade J) took the view that the intention of the client at the material time was pertinent. Accordingly, the 'client intends' is key to whether the task is a single event and/or cumulative.

6.   TUPE in 2014 and Beyond

Anyone involved in TUPE issues will be aware that this is a subject matter which is fast evolving. This chapter seeks to provide general guidance in relation to TUPE issues in light of the changes to TUPE made by the 2014 TUPE Amendment Regulations.

The 1977 ARD did not prove easy to apply in practice, and has been particularly controversial in relation to contracting-out/outsourcing. It has resulted in a significant number of cases being referred from the domestic courts to the ECJ in an effort to obtain clarity as regards its proper interpretation. Although the 1988 Amending Directive (which itself was further revised in the form of a Consolidation Directive) did provide a degree of clarification, a number of uncertainties as regards the practical implications of the TUPE requirements still remain, perhaps most notably:

- the application of TUPE to second stage service provision changes (contracting-out/outsourcing);
- the difficulties of obtaining requisite information regarding TUPE issues from the first contractor on a stage 2 contracting-out (discussed further below);
- dismissals from employment in a TUPE transfer situation, and particularly the applicability of ETO defences to place of work redundancies; and
- harmonisation of post-transfer employment terms and conditions.

In brief:

From January 2014, the Government will have revised TUPE for the third time.

The 2014 TUPE Amendment Regulations do not repeal the service provision change (SPC) rule. Consequently, the pre-existing case law becomes of paramount importance.

Yet, the Government has made an amendment to TUPE 2006 to confirm that, for there to be a service provision change on or after 31 January 2014, the activities carried on post-transfer must be 'fundamentally the same' as those carried on before it. [Regulation 5 of the 2014 TUPE Amendment Regulations inserting a new Regulation 3(2A) in the 2006 TUPE Regulations]

A major shift in line with the UK's Coalition Government's mission to reduce red-tape is to apply a small employers' exemption to TUPE. Consequently, UK employers of 10 or fewer employees with no trade union or employee representative body will be able to inform and consult directly with employees prior to a transfer thus avoiding the need to elect employee representatives.

Prior to the introduction of the 2014 TUPE Amendment Regulations, Regulation 4 of TUPE rendered void any contractual changes where the reason for the change is the transfer itself or a reason connected to the transfer that is not an 'economic, technical or organisational reason entailing changes in the workforce'. In terms of the ETO defence, the Government has, as a consequence of the amendments made by the 2014 TUPE Amendment Regulations, limited this prohibition on contractual changes to changes where the reason for the change is the 'transfer itself'. In other words, the wider prohibition on changes for a reason 'connected to the transfer' has been removed. Accordingly, by extending the circumstances where contracts of employment can be varied and thereby extending the ETO definition, the protective effect of TUPE is diluted. Furthermore, in terms of new Regulation 7, by the removal of the second limb (i.e. 'a reason connected with the transfer'), the Regulation more closely reflects the wording of the Directive. The aim is to reduce the likelihood that TUPE is interpreted more widely than the Directive, and thereby reduce legal risk and provide more clarity. This will effectively create a new test for whether a dismissal is automatically unfair. Both transferor and transferee will be able to share ETO reasons.

The Government has also clarified that a 'static' approach to collective agreements will apply. This means that transferees will be bound by the terms of a collective agreement applying at the date of transfer but will not be bound by future terms and conditions negotiated via collective bargaining to which they are not a party.

In addition, terms deriving from a collective agreement can be re-negotiated one year post-transfer (even where the reason for the change is the transfer itself). The caveat to this, however, is that the overall change must be 'no less favourable'.

Finally, the Government has extended the period prior to the transfer by which the transferor must provide information about the transferring employees from 14 to 28 days. More radically, the transferee will be able to consult pre-transfer, removing the lacuna created by existing case law on the consultation regulations.

6.1. New TUPE

The 2014 TUPE Amendment Regulations amended the 2006 TUPE Regulations with effect from 31 January 2014 (the "Commencement Date"). Below we outline TUPE and the principal amendments made by the 2014 Amendment Regulations:

6.1.1. Types of Transfer

The newly amended TUPE Regulations continue to apply in respect of two types of transfer. First, **Regulation 3(1)(a)** refers to *"the transfer of an undertaking, business or part of an undertaking or business situated immediately before the transfer in the United Kingdom to another person where there is a transfer of an economic entity which retains its identity"*.

An "economic entity" for these purposes is defined under Regulation 3(2) as *"an organised grouping of resources which has the objective of pursuing an economic activity, whether or not that activity is central or ancillary"*.

This reflects wording from the Amending Directive and is intended to codify existing case law; that is, the two stage stable economic entity and retention of business identity test applying the *Spijkers* list of factors, as previously noted in Chapter 2.

Secondly, **Regulation 3(1)(b)** restates the SPC (service provision change) transfer which was created by the TUPE Regulations 2006. Specifically, the Regulation describes a service provision change as a situation in which:

(i) activities cease to be carried out by a person ("a Client") on his own behalf and are carried out instead by another person on the Client's behalf ("a Contractor") – sometimes known as stage 1 contracting-out;

(ii) activities cease to be carried out by a Contractor on a Client's behalf (whether or not those activities had previously been carried out by a Client on his own behalf) and are carried out instead by another person ("a Subsequent Contractor") on the Client's behalf – sometimes known as stage 2 contracting-out; or

(iii) activities cease to be carried out by a Contractor or a Subsequent Contractor on a Client's behalf (whether or not those activities had previously been carried out by the Client on his own behalf) and are carried out instead by the Client on his own behalf – in other words, the "repatriation" of services in-house;

and in which the conditions set out in **Regulation 3(3)** are satisfied.

Regulation 3(2A) (inserted by the 2014 TUPE Amendment Regulations) provides that *"References in paragraph (1)(b) to activities being carried out instead by another person (including the client) are to activities which are* *fundamentally the same as the activities carried out by the person who has ceased to carry them out."*

Regulation 3(2A) applies in relation to TUPE transfers which take place on or after 31 January 2014.

Transfers which fall within the scope of **Regulation 3(1)(a)** or **3(1)(b)** are collectively referred to as "relevant transfers" for the purposes of the TUPE Regulations.

In the first decision under **Regulation 3(1)(b)** the Truro Tribunal in *Thomas-James v. Cornwall CC*[1] decided that there was no 'service provision change' within the meaning of TUPE where it was not possible to identify the entity to which the service provision contract had been transferred.

In a separate case the *EAT in Angel Services Ltd v. Hambley & Kimberley Housing Group*[2] addressed the issue of the fragmentation caused by service provision change. Langstaff J held that a service provision change was capable of occurring and TUPE applied, even where 75% of the work was transferred. Yet as the EAT reminds all practitioners in *GEFCO UK Ltd v. Oates*[3] (HHJ McMullen QC presiding), that Tribunals ought to carry out a multi-factorial approach in reaching their conclusions as to whether there is a transfer or not for the purposes of TUPE.

Regulation 3(3), as before, states that the conditions referred to in **Regulation 3(1)(b)** are that:
(a) before the service provision change
    (i) there is an organised grouping of employees situated immediately before the change in Great Britain which has as its principal purpose the carrying out of the activities concerned on behalf of the Client; and
    (ii) the Client intends that following the service provision change, the activities will be carried out by the transferee other than in connection with a single specific event or task of short term duration; and
(b) the activities concerned do not consist wholly or mainly of the supply of goods for the Client's use.

---

[1] Thomas-James v. Cornwall CC [2008] ET1701021-22

[2] Angel Services Ltd v. Hambley & Kimberley Housing Group [2008] IRLR 682

[3] GEFCO UK Ltd v. Oates [2006] EAT

Regulation 3(4) provides that, subject to the provisions of **Regulation 3(1)**, the TUPE Regulations 2006 apply to transfers which fall within the definitions set out in **Regulation 3(1)** involving:

(a) public and private undertakings engaged in economic activities whether or not they are operating for gain (and so, for example, the Regulations would apply to transfers involving charities);

(b) any type of transfer of service provision change, regardless of whether or not:

   (i) the transfer or service provision change is governed by or arises as a result of the law of any country or territory outside the United Kingdom, or the service provision change is governed or effected by the law of a country or territory outside Great Britain

   (ii) that the employment of any of the transferring employees is governed by any such law. **Regulation 3(4)(c)** provides that the TUPE Regulations 2006 apply to transfers (including service provision change transfers) where the individuals employed in the undertaking (or part) transferred ordinarily work outside the United Kingdom.

It should, however, be noted that **Regulation 3(5)** confirms that an administrational reorganisation of any public administrative authority or the transfer of administration functions between public administrative authorities does not constitute a relevant transfer for the purposes of the Regulations, whilst **Regulation 3(6)** provides that a relevant transfer may be effected by a series of two or more transactions, and may take place whether or not any property is transferred by the transferor to the transferee.

Regulation 3(7) provides that if in consequence (whether directly or indirectly) of a transfer of an undertaking (or part of an undertaking) which immediately before the transfer was situated in the United Kingdom, a UK-registered ship ceases to be UK-registered, the TUPE Regulations do not affect the right (arising under section 5 of the Merchant Shipping Act 1970) of any seaman employed on the ship to be discharged when the ship ceases to be UK-registered.

6.1.2. Effect of Relevant Transfers

Regulation 4(1) provides that save where an employee objects to becoming employed by the transferee, a relevant transfer does not have the effect of terminating the contract of employment of any person employed by the transferor and assigned to the organised grouping of resources or employees that is subject to the transfer, but rather that any such contract shall have effect following the transfer as if originally made between the transferring employee and the transferee. Under **Regulation 4(2)**, (but subject to **Regulation 8** and **Regulation 15(9)**), which are discussed further below) on the completion of relevant transfer:

(a) all the rights, powers, duties and liabilities of the transferor under or in connection with any contract of employment of any transferring employee are transferred to the transferee; and

(b) anything done (or omitted to be done) by or in relation to the transferor before the completion of the relevant transfer occurs in respect of the contract of employment or the transferring employees shall be deemed to have been done (or omitted to have been done) by or in relation to the transferee.

The EAT in *Perry's Motor Sales Ltd v. Lindley*[4] held with regard to Regulation 4 of TUPE Regulations 2006 that:
"The transferor, by its actions prior to the transfer, can, by Regulation 4(2)(b), cause to crystallise, on the transfer, a liability in the transferee, whose actions they are deemed to be, which was not a liability of the transferor prior to the transfer, which does not transfer under 4(2)(a), but which, nonetheless, is a liability of the transferee as the employer of the Claimant".

This, as some commentators suggest, presents a shift away from the previous orthodoxy that TUPE operates to preserve rights accrued on transfer, i.e. which are pre-existing. In contrast, the EAT concluded that the act of transfer itself can vest a liability in the transferee which did not previously exist, and as such **Regulation 4(2)(b)** is not tied to, or limited by, **Regulation 4(2)(a)**. In doing so, the EAT distinguished a series of Court of Appeal decision, including the recent decision of Mummery LJ in *Jackson v Computershare Services*[5].

However, **Regulation 4(2)** does not operate so as to transfer (or otherwise affect) the liability of any person to be prosecuted for, convicted of and sentenced for any offence.

Subject to **Regulation 9** (which addresses variations of contracts when the transferor is subject to insolvency proceedings) any purported variation of a contract of employment that is or will be transferred by **Regulation 4(1)** is void if the sole or principal reason for the variation is the transfer **(Regulation 4(4))** (as amended). However, **Regulation 4(5)** (as amended)

---

[4] Perry's Motor Sales Ltd & Anor v. Lindley [2008] EAT 0616/07

[5] Jackson v Computershare Services [2008] IRLR 70

provides that Regulation 4(4) does not prevent a variation of a contract if the sole or principal reason for the variation is (a) an ETO reason entailing changes in the workforce provided the employer and employee agree the variation, or (b) the terms of the relevant contract permits the employer to make the variation. Further, **Regulation 4(4)** does not apply in respect of a variation of a contract in so far as it varies a term or condition incorporated from a collective agreement, provided that:

(a) the variation of the contract takes effect on a date more than one year after the date of the TUPE transfer; and

(b) following that variation, the rights and obligations in the employee's contract, when considered together, are no less favourable to the employee than those which applied immediately before the variation (**Regulation 4(5B)**).

Regulation 4(5A) (inserted by the 2014 TUPE Amendment Regulations) states that the expression "changes in the workforce" includes a change to the place where employees are employed by the employer to carry on the business of the employer or to carry out work of a particular kind for the employer (and the reference to such a place has the same meaning as in section 139 of the Employment Rights Act 1996). Note that the amendments to Regulation 4 made by the 2014 TUPE Amendment Regulations apply in respect of of transfers made on or after 31 January 2014 (or in a case where a variation is not agreed, it starts to have effect on or after that date).

Regulation 4(8) provides that, subject to **Regulations 4(9)** and **4(11)** if an employee objects to the transfer of his employment to a transferee under a relevant transfer, the relevant transfer operates so as to terminate his contract of employment with the transferor; moreover, the employee is not treated, for any purpose, as having been dismissed by the transferor. However, (subject to **Regulation 9**, which addresses variations of contracts where the transferor is subject to relevant insolvency proceedings, as previously noted in Chapter 4) where a relevant transfer involves a "substantial change" in working conditions to the detriment of a person who would otherwise be a transferring employee, the employee may, under **Regulation 4(9)**, treat the contract of employment as having been terminated, and the employee in such circumstances is treated (for any purpose) as having been dismissed by the transferor. No damages will be payable by an employer as a result of a dismissal falling within Regulation 4(9) in respect of any failure by the employer to pay wages to an employee in respect of a notice period which the employee has failed to work. **Regulation 4(11)** specifies that **Regulations 4(1), 4(7), 4(8),** and **4(9)** are without prejudice to any right of an employee (arising other than under the

TUPE Regulations 2006) to terminate his employment contract without notice in acceptance of a repudiatory breach by his employer. This provision clearly restates the role of the ET as a fact-finding body. Consequently, an ET will be charged with the task of analysing, as it does for 'SOSR' (some other substantial reason) in respect of unfair dismissals, as to whether the transfer has initiated little or substantial change, applying the existing case law, as discussed in Chapter 2.

6.1.3. Collective Agreements and Trade Union Recognition

If, at the time of the making of a relevant transfer, there exists a collective agreement (as defined for the purposes of the Trade Union and Labour Relations (Consolidation) Act 1992) made by (or on behalf of) the transferor and a recognised trade union in respect of any employee transferring pursuant to the relevant transfer, **Regulation 5** provides that following the transfer, the collective agreement shall have effect as if made by (or on behalf of) the transferee and the trade union in respect of the relevant transferring employee.

However, **Regulation 4A(1)** of the TUPE Regulations 2006 (inserted by the 2014 TUPE Amendment Regulations) provides (in respect of transfers that take place pursuant to Regulation 4(1) and on or after 31 January 2014) that where a contract of employment incorporates provisions of collective agreements, **Regulation 4(2)** does not transfer any rights, powers, duties and liabilities in relation to any provision of a collective agreement if:

(a) the provision of the collective agreement is agreed after the date of the TUPE transfer; and

(b) the transferee employer is not a participant to the collective agreement for that provision.

Regulation 4A(2) confirms that the contract of employment has effect after the transfer as if it does not incorporate provisions of a collective agreement which meet the conditions of **Regulation 4A(1)**.

Regulation 6 relates to trade union recognition in circumstances where the transferred organised grouping of resources or transferred employees remain distinct from the remainder of the transferee's undertaking. In such circumstances, if before the making of the relevant transfer, an independent trade union was recognised to any extent by the transferor in respect of any of the transferring employees, then following the transfer, the union shall be deemed to have been recognised by the transferee to the same extent as the union had previously been recognised by the transferor (in relation to the relevant transferring employees) and any agreement for recognition may be varied or rescinded accordingly [cf. *TGWU v. Swissport*[6]]. Such might include subsequent changes to collective agreements (*Worrall & others v. Wilmott Dixon Partnership*[7]).

6.1.4. Employee Dismissal

The 2014 TUPE Amendment Regulations amend **Regulations 7(1) to (3)** of TUPE 2006 in respect of TUPE transfers that take place on or after 31 January 2014, and the date when any notice of termination is given by an employer or an employee in respect of of any dismissal is 31 January 2014 or later, or in a case where no notice is give, the date on which the termination takes effect is 31 January 2014 or later.

If an employee of the transferor or the transferee is dismissed, whether before or after the making of a relevant transfer, **Regulation 7(1)** provides that the employee will be treated as having been unfairly dismissed for the purposes of Part 10 of the ERA if the reason for the dismissal was the transfer itself. Regulation 7(1) does not, however, apply to dismissals that may take place solely or principally for economic, technical or organisational reasons entailing changes in the workforce of either the transferor or transferee before or after the relevant transfer (**Regulation 7(2)**) and **7(3)(a).**

Regulation 7(3)(b) provides, that if a dismissal takes place for a reason specified in **Regulation 7(2)**, without prejudice to the application of section 98(4)(2) of the ERA, for the purposes of sections 98(1) and 135 of the ERA (reason for dismissal):

(a) the dismissal is to be regarded as having been for a redundancy where section 98(2)(c) of the ERA applies; or

(b) in any other case, the dismissal is regarded as having been for a substantial reason of a kind such as to justify the dismissal of an employee holding the position that the employee held.

6.1.5. Insolvency

As discussed in Chapter 4, **Regulation 8** excludes certain insolvency proceedings from the application of transfer-related liabilities and unfair dismissal, and addresses the issue of where the liability for pre-existing debts owed to transferring employees falls. **Regulation 9** (as amended) addresses the issue of variations to terms and conditions of employment in

---

[6] Transport & General Workers Union v. Swissport(UK) Ltd & anor [2007], EAT 0603

[7] Worrall & others v. Wilmott Dixon Partnership [2010] EAT/0521/09

connection with relevant transfers in respect of insolvent businesses, subject to certain safeguards.

6.1.6. Pensions

Regulation 10(1) disapplies **Regulations 4** and **5**:

(a) to so much of a contract of employment or collective agreement as relates to an occupational pension scheme; or

(b) to any rights, powers, duties or other liabilities under or in connection with any such contract of subsisting by virtue of any such agreement and relating to a scheme or otherwise arising in connection with that pension's employment and relating to such a scheme. **Regulation 10(3)** states that any provisions of an occupational pension scheme, which do not relate to benefits for old age, invalidity or survivors shall be treated as not being part of the scheme (and hence are capable, in principle, of passing upon the making of a relevant transfer).

The pensions aspects of TUPE are discussed in greater detail in Chapter 3.

6.1.7. Employee Liability Information

Regulation 11(2) of the TUPE Regulations defines "employee liability information" as:

(a) the identity and age of the employee;

(b) the particulars of employment which an employer is obliged to provide to an employee under section 1 of the ERA;

(c) information of (i) any disciplinary procedure taken against an employee, and (ii) any grievance procedure taken by an employee, in both cases within the previous two years, where a Code of Practice issued under Part IV of the Trade Union and Labour Relations (Consolidation) Act 1992 which relates exclusively or primarily to the resolution of disputes apply;

(d) information of any court or tribunal case, claim or action (i) brought by an employee against the transferor, within the previous two years, or (ii) that the transferor has reasonable grounds to believe that an employee may bring against the transferee arising out of the employee's employment with the transferor; and

(e) information of any collective agreement which will have effect in relation to the transferring employer under **Regulation 5(a)**.

Regulation 11(1) requires the transferor to notify the transferee (in writing) of the employer liability information relating to each transferring employee, or make that information available to the transferee in a readily accessible form. The notification (in respect of TUPE transfers made on or after 1 May 2014) must be given not less than 28 days (14 days if the TUPE transfer occurs before 1 May 2014) before the relevant transfer or (if special circumstances mean that this is not reasonably practicable, as soon as reasonably practicable thereafter). Notification may be provided in more than one instalment, and indirectly, via a third party (for example, the transferor's legal advisers) (**Regulation 11(6)** as amended).

Employer liability information must contain information as at a specified date (being not more than 14 days before the date on which the information is notified or otherwise made available to the transferee); the transferor is also under a duty to notify the transferee in writing of any changes to the employee liability information which may arise after the information has initially been provided (**Regulation 11(3)**).

Regulation 12 sets out penalties for failure by the transferor to comply with the employee liability information requirements. In particular, the transferee may complain before an employment tribunal (on or after the date of the relevant transfer) that the transferor has failed to comply with its obligations in relation to the employee liability information notification requirements. Any such complaint must be brought before the end of the period of three months beginning with the date of the relevant transfer, or within such longer period as the tribunal considers reasonable when the tribunal is satisfied that it was not reasonably practicable for the complaint to be brought within the three month period.

If the ET finds the complaint to be well-founded, it will make a declaration to this effect, and may order that compensation be paid by the transferor to the transferee. The amount of compensation must be such amount as the tribunal considers just and equitable in all the circumstances, having regard to the loss suffered by the transferee in relation to the failure of the transferor, and any contractual arrangements between the employers as regards any failure by the transferor to notify the transferee of the employee liability information. However (and subject to the general duty upon claimants to mitigate any loss as it applies to the calculation of damages claims), any compensation awarded by the tribunal will not be less than £1000 in respect of each employee to which the transferor's failure relates unless the tribunal considers it just and equitable having regard to all the circumstances, to award a lesser sum.

6.1.8. Duty to Inform and Consult

Regulation 13(1) introduces the concept of "affected employees", who are any employees of the transferor or the transferee (whether or not they themselves are employed in the relevant organised grouping of resources, or are otherwise transferring employees) who may be affected by the relevant transfer or may be affected by measures taken in relation to the transfer (cf. *Adult Learning Inspectorate v. Beloff*[8]).

Regulation 13(2) provides that, long enough before a relevant transfer to enable the employer of any affected employers to consult all the appropriate representatives of any of the affective employers, the employer must inform the representatives:

(a) that the relevant transfer is to take place, the date (or proposed date) of the transfer and the reasons for making the transfer;

(b) the legal, economic and social implications in respect of the affected employees;

(c) the measure which the employer envisages will, in connection with the transfer, be taken in relation to the affected employees (or, if in fact the employer envisages that no measures will be taken, that this is the case); and

(d) (if the employer is the transferor) the measures in relation to the relevant transfer which it envisages will be taken by the transferee in respect of those affected employees who will become the transferee's employees following the completion of the transfer (or if the employer envisages that no such measures will be taken, the employer must inform the representatives of that fact (*Cable Realisations Ltd v. GMB Northern*[9]).

The transferee is obliged, under **Regulation 13(4)**, to give the transferor such information at such time as will enable the transferor to perform the duties referred to in paragraph (d) above.

Regulation 13(2A) (inserted from 1 October 2011 by the Agency Workers Regulations 2010 (SI 2010/93)) provides that where information is to be supplied under Regulation 13(2) by an employer –

(a) this must include suitable information relating to the use of agency workers (if any) by that employer; and

(b) "suitable information relating to the use of agency workers" means:

(i) the number of agency workers temporarily for an under the supervision and direction of the employer;

(ii) the parts of the employer's undertaking in which those agency workers are working; and

(iii) the type of work those agency workers are carrying out.

---

[8] Adult Learning Inspectorate v. Beloff [2007] EAT/0238/07

[9] Cable Realisations Ltd v. GMB Northern [2010] ICR 902

The 2014 TUPE Amendment Regulations insert **Regulation 13A** into the TUPE Regulations 2006, (in respect of TUPE transfers which take place on or after 31 July 2014) relating to "micro-businesses". **Regulation 13A** provides that if, at the time when the employer is required to give information under **Regulation 13(2)**, the employer employs fewer than 10 employees, there are no appropriate representatives within the meaning of **Regulation 13(3)** (see below) and the employer has not invited any of the affected employees to elect employee representatives, the employer may comply with **Regulation 13** by performing any duty which relates to appropriate representatives as if each of the affected employees were an appropriate representative.

Regulation 13(3) provides that the appropriate representatives of any employees are (if any of the employees are members of a recognised independent trade union) representatives of the relevant trade union, or otherwise whichever of the following employee representatives the employer chooses:

(a) employee representatives appointed or elected by the affected employee (otherwise than for the purposes of Regulation 13) who have the requisite authority from the employees to receive information and to be consulted in relation to the proposed transfer in respect of the relevant affected employees; and

(b) employee representatives elected by the affected employees for the purposes of the Regulations in an election which satisfies the requirements of **Regulation 14(1)**.

Regulation 13(5) requires that information provided to the appropriate representatives must be given to the them personally, or sent by post to an address notified by them to the employer or (in the case of trade union representatives) sent by post to the union at its head or main office.

If an employer of any affected employees anticipates that in relation to the transfer, it will be taking measures in relation to any such employee, it is obliged, under **Regulation 13(6)**, to consult with all the appropriate representatives of the employee and to seek their agreement to the measures which are to be taken. As part of the consultation exercise, the employer is obliged under **Regulation 13(7)** to consider any representations made by the appropriate representatives, to reply to such representations and if the employer does not accept such representations the employer is obliged to state its reasons for rejecting them.

Regulation 13(8) provides that the employer is also obliged to allow the appropriate representatives access to the affected employees, and to provide the representatives such accommodation and other facilities as may be appropriate.

If there are special circumstances which mean that it will not be reasonably practicable for the employer to perform any of the duties imposed as a result of **Regulations 13(2)** to **13(7)**, the employer is obliged, as a result of **Regulation 13(9)**, to take all such steps towards performing the relevant duty as are reasonably practicable in the circumstances.

The obligations imposed on an employer by **Regulation 13** will apply irrespective of whether the decision resulting in the relevant transfer is taken by the employer, or by a person controlling the employer.

6.1.9. Election of Employee Representatives

As we have noted above, **Regulation 13(3)** envisages the possibility of affected employees electing employee representatives for the purposes of the Regulations. **Regulation 14(1)** sets out the requirements for the election of the employee representatives, which are that:

(a) the employer must make such arrangements as are reasonably practicable so that the election is fair;

(b) the employer has the responsibility of deciding the number of representatives to be elected. However, there must be sufficient representatives to represent the interests of all the affected employees having regard to the number and classes of those employees;

(c) the employer has the responsibility of deciding whether the representatives should represent all of the affected employees, or whether particular classes of affected employees should be represented by different representatives;

(d) prior to the election being held, the employer must determine the term of office of the employee representatives, and it must be of sufficient length so as to enable information to be provided and the consultation exercise to be carried out;

(e) the candidates for election as employee representatives must be affected employees on the date of the election;

(f) no affected employee can be unreasonably excluded from standing as a candidate for the post of employee representative;

(g) all affected employees on the date of the election must be entitled to vote in the election;

(h) the affected employee must be permitted to vote for as many candidates as there are representatives to be elected to represent them (or, if there are to be representatives for particular classes of employees, must be permitted to vote for as many candidates as there are representatives to be elected for their particular class); and

(i) the election must be conducted in such a way that, so far as is reasonably practicable, the vote is by secret ballot, and the votes cast are accurately counted.

If the employer invites any of the affected employees to elect employee representatives and the invitation was issued long enough before the time when the employer is required to provide information under **Regulation 13(2)** so as to allow them to elect representatives by that time, the employer shall be treated as complying with the requirements of **Regulation 13** if it complies with the requirements as soon as is reasonably practicable after the representatives are in fact elected.

Moreover, if the employer invites affected employees to elect representatives, and they fail to do so within a reasonably time, the employer is obliged (under **Regulation 13(11)**) to give each affected employee the information specified in **Regulation 13(2)**.

Regulation 14(2) provides that if an election of employee representatives has been held, and one of those representatives subsequently ceases to act so as to cause any of the employees to no longer be represented, the employees shall elect another representative by an election satisfying the prescribed requirements.

6.1.10. Failure to Inform or Consult

Regulation 15(1) provides that failure by an employer to comply with the information and consultation requirements of **Regulations 13** or **14** can lead to a complaint being brought before an employment tribunal:

(a) if the complaint relates to a failure in respect of the election of employee representatives, by any of the affected employees;

(b) if the complaint relates to any other failure in respect of the employee representatives, by any of the employee representatives to whom the failure related;

(c) if the complaint relates to any failure in respect of representatives of a trade union, by the trade union; and

(d) if the complaint relates to any other matter, by any of the affected employees. If a complaint is brought, and the issue arises as to whether or not it was reasonably practicable for the employer to perform a particular duty or as to what steps it took towards performing it, **Regulation 15(2)** provides that it is for the employer to demonstrate that there were special circumstances which meant that it was not reasonably practicable for the employer to perform the particular duty and that it took all such steps towards its performance as were reasonably practicable in those circumstances.

Moreover, if a complaint is brought and the question arises as to whether or not any employee representative was an appropriate representative for the purposes of **Regulation 10**, it is the employer's responsibility to demonstrate that the employee representative had the requisite authority to represent the affected employees (except in respect of TUPE transfers which occur on or after 31 July 2014, where the question is whether or not **Regulation 13A** applied). If there is a query as to whether the election requirements of the **Regulation 14** were satisfied, it is again the employer's responsibility to demonstrate that this was the case.

If on a complaint under **Regulation 15(1)** a question arises as to whether or not **Regulation 13A** applied, it is for the employer to show that it employed fewer than 10 members and there were no appropriate representatives (within the meaning of **Regulation 13(3)**) at the relevant time referred to in **Regulation 13A(1)**. [**Regulation 15(3A)** of the TUPE Regulations 2006 as inserted by **Regulation 11(4)** of the 2014 TUPE Amendment Regulations].

If a complaint is brought against the transferor alleging that it has failed to carry out the duty imposed as a result of **Regulation 13(2)(d)** (the obligation to provide information as to the measures that the transferee envisages it will take in respect of the affected employees post-transfer), or (where applicable) **Regulation 13(9)** (the obligation to take all such steps towards performing a relevant duty as are reasonably practicable having regard to any special circumstances which may apply), the transferor may not rely upon the excuse that it was not reasonably practicable for it to perform the relevant duty simply because the transferee had failed to provide the requisite information at the relevant time unless the transferor has given the transferee notice of its intention to advance such an argument. The provision of such notice automatically makes the transferee a party to the proceedings.

It should also be noted that the failure on the part of any party directly or indirectly controlling the employer to provide requisite information to the employer will not constitute special circumstances rendering it not reasonably practicable for the employer to comply with such a requirement.

If a complaint against a transferee is found to be well-founded by the tribunal, the tribunal will make a declaration to this effect and may, under **Regulation 15(7)**, order the transferee to pay "appropriate compensation" to such affected employees as the tribunal may specify.

If a complaint against a transferor is found to be well-founded, the tribunal will make an appropriate declaration and may, under **Regulation 15(8)(a)** order the transferor (subject to **Regulation 15(9)**) to pay appropriate compensation to the relevant affected employees. However, if the complaint is that the transferor did not carry out the duties imposed upon it under **Regulation 13(2)(d)** or **Regulation 13(9)**, and the transferor (after giving appropriate notice) demonstrates that the failure occurred as a result of the failure by the transferee to provide the requisite information, **Regulation 15(8)(b)** provides that the tribunal may order the transferee to pay appropriate compensation to the relevant affected employees.

If a tribunal orders that appropriate compensation should be paid, an employee can bring a complaint before an employment tribunal if he believes that he falls within the description of affected employees to whom compensation should be paid in accordance with the terms of the order but in respect of whom no compensation has in fact been paid. **Regulation 15(11)** provides that if the tribunal finds the employee's complaint to be well-founded, the tribunal can order the transferor or the transferee (as appropriate) to pay the complainant the amount of compensation which the tribunal determines is due to him.

The transferee and the transferor are jointly and severally liable in respect of any compensation payable as a result of orders issued under **Regulation 15(8)(a)** or **15(11)**.

"Appropriate compensation" in **Regulation 15** is defined (in **Regulation 16(3)**) as meaning such sum not exceeding 13 weeks' pay for the employee in question as the tribunal considers just and equitable having regard to the seriousness of the employer's failure to comply with its duty (*Susie Radin Ltd v. GMB*).[10]

Sections 220 to 228 of the ERA shall apply when calculating the amount that constitutes a week's pay for any employee for the purposes of **Regulation 16(3)**, and for the purposes of that calculation, the calculation date will be:
(a) in respect of an employee who is dismissed by reason of redundancy, the date which is the calculation date for the purposes of any entitlement on the part of the employee to a redundancy payment (or which would have been that calculation date if he were so entitled);

---

[10] Susie Radin Ltd v. GMB [2004] ICR 893

(b) in respect of any employee who is dismissed for any other reason, the effective date on which his contract of employment was terminated; and

(c) in any other case, the date of the relevant transfer.

Complaints must be presented to an employment tribunal before the end of the three month period beginning:

(a) on the date on which the relevant transfer is completed (in respect of a complaint brought under **Regulation 15(1)**); or

(b) on the date of the tribunal's order issued under **Regulations 15(7)** or **15(8)** in respect of any complaint brought under **Regulation 15(8)**, or within such longer period as the tribunal considers reasonable when it is satisfied that it was not reasonably practicable for the complaint to be brought within the three months period.

Appeals against an order issued by an employment tribunal in respect of any order issued under Regulation 15 may only be brought before the EAT on a question of law arising from any decision of, or arising in respect of any proceedings before, an employment tribunal and Regulation 6(2) specifically disapplies section 11(1) of the Tribunals and Inquiries Act 1992 (appeals from certain tribunals to the High Court) in relation to any such proceedings.

6.1.11. Employers' Liability Compulsory Insurance

Regulation 17 addresses the issue of compulsory employer insurance. If, as a result of section 3(1)(a) or (b) of the Employers' Liability (Compulsory Insurance) Act 1969, the transferor is not required by that Act to effect any such insurance, or if as a result of section 3(1)(c) of that Act, the transferor is exempt from the requirement to effect insurance under the Act, on the completion of a relevant transfer, the transferee and the transferor will be jointly and severally liable in respect of any liability referred to in section 1(1) of the Employers' Liability (Compulsory Insurance) Act 1969 insofar as such liability relates to the employee's term of service with the transferor before the relevant transfer.

6.1.12. Restriction on Contracting Out

Regulation 18 provides that section 203 of the ERA 1996 (i.e. any provision is void if it purports to exclude or limit any statutory provision, such as TUPE) shall apply to the TUPE Regulations 2006 as if they were contained in that Act. However, that section does not apply insofar as the TUPE Regulations 2006 provide for an agreement (whether or not a contract of employment) to exclude or limit the operation of the Regulations.

6.2.   TUPE and Business Transactions

A business transfer is the transfer of the assets and operations of a business, and is distinct from a transaction involving the sale of the shares of companies. In any business transfer, there are in effect three distinct stages:

(a) information exchange and the identification of legal-HR and other commercial issues of importance relating to the transactions (generally known as the "due diligence process");

(b) drafting, negotiating and ultimately agreeing to the sale and purchase agreement (and any other relevant legal documents); and

(c) conclusion of the sale (i.e. executing the sale and purchase agreement and completing the transaction.

6.3.   Due Diligence

It is clearly of importance to the prospective buyer of a business that he gains as much information as possible about the target business, so that he can gain as clear as possible an understanding of the value of the assets and liabilities he will be acquiring, and will be able to gauge as far as is possible whether the prospective purchase price is acceptable having regard to all relevant circumstances. This being the case, most (but by no means all) transactions usually commence with a due diligence exercise following the agreement of "heads of terms" between the parties setting out the broad parameters of the prospective transaction.

In practice, the complexity of modern business transactions means that the due diligence exercise often continues even whilst the legal and commercial terms of the sale and purchase agreement are under negotiation, with the stream of results from the due diligence exercise impacting upon the negotiation of such terms, as a better understanding of the target business is developed by the prospective buyer.

The due diligence exercise will, of course, generally cover all aspects of the target business, and the exercise generally commences with the buyer (or more typically its advisers) providing the seller with a due diligence questionnaire setting out a series of preliminary questions relating to the business. Answers (or non-answers) to those questions can, in turn, lead to other questions being asked. On occasions (especially in bid situations), the seller may itself commission a preliminary due diligence report into the affairs of the target business which will be provided to the buyer at the commencement of the transaction.

So far as the employment and pensions aspects of the due diligence exercise are concerned, the due diligence questionnaire will seek to ascertain answers to questions such as:

- Who is the current employer of the employees "working" in the target business? Typically, this will be the seller of the assets of the business, but it may be that the employees are actually employed by another company (for example, a service company) within the seller's corporate group;

- Which employees will transfer under TUPE as a result of the proposed transaction? In this regard, the buyer will wish to identify whether any employees who will transfer are presently on sick leave, maternity leave, secondment or otherwise temporarily absent from work;

- What are the terms of the employees' contracts of employment? Are there any unusual provisions, for example, unusual notice periods, higher than anticipated salary entitlements, or any restrictive covenants which may provide to be unenforceable? What type of employee benefit arrangements do the employees enjoy? In particular, are there any arrangements (for example, share option arrangements) which could prove difficult for the buyer to replicate in their entirety?

- Has the seller already commenced its consultation exercise, and if so, what information has been provided to the employees and/or their representatives. If the consultation exercise has not yet commenced, what are the seller's intentions in this regard, and how will this correlate with the buyer's intentions in this respect?

- Have any employees registered objections to the proposed transfer? If so, what are the grounds for such objections?

- How will the seller comply with its obligations in relation to the provision of employee liability information?

- Have there been any dismissals of employees? In this regard, it should be noted that it is not unknown for some sellers to dismiss or otherwise purport to alter the terms of employees working in the target business in order to make the business more attractive to prospective buyers, for example, in order to reduce perceived labour costs (this may be the case where receivers or liquidators are involved). It is important to stress that in the event of any claim being brought before an employment tribunal as a result of any such actions by the seller, the tribunal will focus upon the reason for the dismissal, rather than the timing of the dismissal in respect of the transfer. However, inferences in relation to the connection to the transfer (whether past or pending) may be drawn in certain circumstances.

- What are the pension entitlements of the employees? For example, do they enjoy membership of personal pension schemes (rights which would pass upon the making of the transfer) or membership of an occupational pension scheme?

- Even if the employees enjoy membership of an occupational pension scheme, is it intended that the scheme should be passed to the buyer so that continued membership can be enjoyed? (If this is the case, the buyer will no doubt require a detailed analysis of the pension scheme, in particular as regards it funding status (if it is a final salary pension scheme) and its compliance with legal and regulatory requirements).
- Have all pension contributions which have fallen due been paid?
- Is there any possibility of the buyer becoming liable as a result of *Beckmann/Martin* liabilities passing, notwithstanding the existence of the TUPE pensions exclusion discussed in Chapter 3? In this regard, the buyer will be concerned not only in relation to any *Beckmann/Martin* liabilities which may pass as a result of membership of any pension scheme operated by the seller, but also in respect of membership of any "historic" pension schemes, and which may have passed to the seller as a result of earlier TUPE transfers resulting in the employees (or at least some of them) passing into the employment of the seller. (The possibility of historic TUPE transfers can often pose difficulties in transactions, since it is often difficult for sellers to provide complete reassurance as to whether or not *Beckmann/Martin* liabilities could have passed as a result. This is an area which can require sellers and buyers to reach a commercial view as to the risks involved, rather than obtaining crystal clear legal certainty as to the risks).

6.4.   Negotiation of the Contractual Terms

Negotiation of the contractual terms will inevitably depend upon the data obtained as a result of the due diligence exercise. The buyer will seek to obtain the benefit of warranties in the sale and purchase agreement whereby the seller will provide legally-binding representations as regards matters relating the target business and its operation; for example, that the seller has accurately disclosed details of the employees to be transferred, (including their terms of employment) and details of any relevant pension schemes. Conversely, the seller will wish to limit its potential exposure as regards the provision of warranties, and the parties may want to debate whether the warranty protection being sought is appropriate to the nature of the transaction.

The effect of warranties may be limited or altered as a result of the due diligence exercise. In addition to the possibility that the legal efficacy of any particular warranty may be affected by information provided as a result of the due diligence exercise, there is likely to be a "disclosure letter" whereby specific declarations of fact are made against specific warranties, with the effect that any particular warranty should be read in conjunction with any specific disclosure made against the warranty.

The terms of any specific disclosures should be the subject of negotiation and agreement between the parties in the same manner as the warranties themselves.

In addition to the warranties and the disclosure letter, the sale and purchase documentation may include a "pensions schedule" if it is intended that the buyer should assume responsibility for the seller's (occupational) pension scheme or if the transaction involves any form of enhanced transfer payment being made from the seller's pension scheme to the buyer's pension scheme. Enhanced transfer payments were commonly found in TUPE transfer situations in the 1990s, but have become far less common in recent years. Nevertheless, if the circumstances of the transaction require the making of any enhanced transfer payment, both sides will require the services of experienced actuaries who will assist in the negotiation of the terms of the schedule alongside the legal advisers working on the transaction.

The sale and purchase agreement is also likely to contain a number of indemnities, whereby one party to the transaction agrees to indemnify the other party against any costs and/or other liabilities that the other party may incur or suffer as a result of any particular event or set of circumstances. In the context of a TUPE transfer, it would be typical for the seller to indemnify the buyer against any liabilities arising in respect of employment before the transfer date; similarly, the buyer will usually indemnify the seller against employment liabilities arising in respect of the post-transfer period. Care should be taken when negotiating such indemnities to ensure that one party does not inadvertently become responsible for liabilities which were not intended (or anticipated) to become the responsibility of that party. For example, any indemnity provided by the seller should be scrutinised to ensure it does not inadvertently make the seller responsible for any *Beckmann/Martin* liabilities arising in respect of the post-transfer period when this was not intended (as would usually be the case).

6.5.   Other issues

We have already discussed the consultation requirements arising under the TUPE Regulations 2006. These requirements impose obligations on both seller and buyer and ideally, any consultation exercises with affected employees by the two parties will be conducted so as to "dovetail" neatly; i.e. so that there are no discrepancies in the information being provided to the employees by the seller and the buyer. This will require clear channels of communication between the seller and the buyer in this regard.

In addition, (and this will no doubt be a matter which will be addressed in the consultation exercise), the buyer must be prepared to ensure that adequate replacement pension provision is provided for the transferring employees following the making of the TUPE transfer, so as to satisfy the requirements of the Pension Protection Regulations discussed in Chapter 3. In this regard, it may be that a period of time elapses between the transfer date and the date on which a replacement pension scheme can be established. If this is the case, it would be usual for the transferring employees to be offered "membership" of the replacement scheme which is "backdated" to the transfer date.

Further References

Bourn *et al.*, *The Transfer of Undertakings in the Public Sector*, (1999) Dartmouth: Aldershot.

Cavalier, *Transfer Rights: TUPE in Perspective*, (1997) Institute of Employment Rights: London.

Derbyshire, Butterfill & Hardy, "Transfer Troubles" *Chartered Secretary* (2004).

Derbyshire and Richards, Business Transfers – New regulations expected in April, *BVCA Technical Bulletin*, Issue 32, (January 2006).

Derbyshire & Hardy, New TUPE 2006, *Pensions Management*, February 2006.

Derbyshire & Hardy, *Pensions and Employment Law: Issues at the Interface*, Sweet & Maxwell, 2008.

Hardy, The Acquired Rights Directive: A Case of Economic and Social Rights at Work, Chapter 24 in *Collins, Davies and Rideout (eds.) on legal Regulation of the Employment Relation*, (2001) Kluwer : Netherlands.

Hardy, Understanding TUPE, (2001) Chandos: Oxford.

Hardy & Adnett, Entrepreneurial Freedom versus employee rights: the Acquired Rights Directive and EU Social Policy post-Amsterdam, (1999) *Journal of European Social Policy*, SAGE: London.

Hardy & Painter, The New Acquired Rights Directive and its Implications for European Employee Relations in the Twenty-First Century, (1999) *Maastricht Journal of European and Comparative Law*, METRO: Netherlands.

Harvey, *Harvey on Industrial Relations and Employment Law*, (Division F), (2010) Butterworths: London.

IDS Handbook – TUPE, May 2007.

McMullen, *Business Transfers and Employee Rights* (2000) Butterworths: London.

Napier, CCT, *Market Testing and Employment Right: The effects of TUPE and the Acquired Rights Directive*, (1993) Institute of Employment Rights: London.

Useful Websites & Social Media

For BIS information on TUPE see: www.bis.gov.uk

For *'Staff Transfers in the Public Sector: Statement of Practice, January 2000'* see: www.cabinet.office.gov.uk/civilservice/2000/tupe

Twitter feeds

@UKELA_LAW

@LexisUK_Employ

@TribunalWatch

@emplawuk

APPENDIX 1: COUNCIL DIRECTIVE 98/50/EC

COUNCIL DIRECTIVE 98/50/EC of 29 June 1998 amending Directive 77/187/EEC on the approximation of the laws of the Member States relating to the safeguarding of employees' rights in the event of transfers of undertakings, businesses or parts of businesses

THE COUNCIL OF THE EUROPEAN UNION,

Having regard to the Treaty establishing the European Community, and in particular Article 100 thereof,

Having regard to the proposal from the Commission (1),

Having regard to the opinion of the European Parliament (2),

Having regard to the opinion of the Economic and Social Committee (3),

Having regard to the opinion of the Committee of the Regions (4),

(1) Whereas the Community Charter of the fundamental social rights of workers adopted on 9 December 1989 ('Social Charter') states, in points 7, 17 and 18 in particular that: 'The completion of the internal market must lead to an improvement in the living and working conditions of workers in the European Community. The improvement must cover, where necessary, the development of certain aspects of employment regulations such as procedures for collective redundancies and those regarding bankruptcies.

Information, consultation and participation for workers must be developed along appropriate lines, taking account of the practices in force in the various Member States. Such information, consultation and participation must be implemented in due time, particularly in connection with restructuring operations in undertakings or in cases of mergers having an impact on the employment of workers;

(2) Whereas Directive 77/187/EEC (5) promotes the harmonisation of the relevant national laws ensuring the safeguarding of the rights of employees and requiring transferors and transferees to inform and consult employees' representatives in good time;

(3) Whereas the purpose of this Directive is to amend Directive 77/187/EEC in the light of the impact of the internal market, the legislative tendencies of the Member States with regard to the rescue of undertakings in economic difficulties, the case-law of the Court of Justice of the European Communities.

Council Directive 75/129/EEC of 17 February 1975 on the approximation of the laws of the Member States relating to collective redundancies (6) and the legislation already in force in most Member States;

(4) Whereas considerations of legal security and transparency require that the legal concept of transfer be clarified in the light of the case-law of the Court of Justice; whereas such clarification does not alter the scope of Directive 77/187/EEC as interpreted by the Court of Justice;

(5) Whereas those considerations also require an express provision, in the light of the case-law of the Court of Justice, that Directive 77/187/EEC should apply to private and public undertakings carrying out economic activities, whether or not they operate for gain;

(6) Whereas it is necessary to clarify the concept of 'employee' in the light of the case-law of the Court of Justice;

(7) Whereas, with a view to ensuring the survival of insolvent undertakings, Member States should be expressly allowed not to apply Articles 3 and 4 of Directive 77/187/EEC to transfers effected in the framework of liquidation proceedings, and certain derogations from that Directive's general provisions should be permitted in the case of transfers effected in the context of insolvency proceedings;

(8) Whereas such derogations should also be allowed for one Member State which has special procedures to promote the survival of companies declared to be in a state of economic crisis;

(9) Whereas the circumstances in which the function and status of employee representatives are to be preserved should be clarified;

(10) Whereas, in order to ensure equal treatment for similar situations, it is necessary to ensure that the information and consultation requirements laid down in Directive 77/187/EEC are complied with irrespective of whether the decision leading to the transfer is taken by the employer or by an undertaking controlling the employer;

(11) Whereas it is appropriate to clarify that, when Member States adopt measures to ensure that the transferee is informed of all the rights and obligations to be transferred, failure to provide that information is not to affect the transfer of the rights and obligations concerned;

(12) Whereas it is necessary to clarify the circumstances in which employees must be informed where there are no employee representatives;

(13) Whereas the Social Charter recognises the importance of the fight against all forms of discrimination, especially based on sex, colour, race, opinion and creed,

HAS ADOPTED THIS DIRECTIVE:

Article 1 Directive 77/187/EEC is hereby amended as follows:

1. the title shall be replaced by the following:

"Council Directive 77/187/EEC of 14 February 1977 on the approximation of the laws of the Member States relating to the safeguarding of employees' rights in the event of transfers of undertakings, businesses or parts of undertakings or businesses";

2. Articles 1 to 7 shall be replaced by the following:

SECTION I
Scope and definitions
Article 1

1.   (a) This Directive shall apply to any transfer of an undertaking, business, or part of an undertaking or business to another employer as a result of a legal transfer or merger.

    (b) Subject to subparagraph (a) and the following provisions of this Article, there is a transfer within the meaning of this Directive where there is a transfer of an economic entity which retains its identity, meaning an organised grouping of resources which has the objective of pursuing an economic activity, whether or not that activity is central or ancillary.

    (c) This Directive shall apply to public and private undertakings engaged in economic activities whether or not they are operating for gain. An administrative reorganisation of public administrative authorities, or the transfer of administrative functions between public administrative authorities, is not a transfer within the meaning of this Directive.

1. This Directive shall apply where and insofar as the undertaking, business or part of the undertaking or business to be transferred is situated within the territorial scope of the Treaty.

2. This Directive shall not apply to sea-going vessels.

Article 2

1. For the purposes of this Directive:

    (a) 'transferor' shall mean any natural or legal person who, by reason of a transfer within the meaning of Article 1(1), ceases to be the employer in respect of the undertaking, business or part of the undertaking or business;

    (b) 'transferee' shall mean any natural or legal person who, by reason of a transfer within the meaning of Article 1(1), becomes the employer in respect of the undertaking, business or part of the undertaking or business;

(c) 'representatives of employees' and related expressions shall mean the representatives of the employees provided for by the laws or practices of the Member States;

(d) 'employee' shall mean any person who, in the Member State concerned, is protected as an employee under national employment law.

2. This Directive shall be without prejudice to national law as regards the definition of contract of employment or employment relationship.

However, Member States shall not exclude from the scope of this Directive contracts of employment or employment relationships solely because:

(a) of the number of working hours performed or to be performed,

(b) they are employment relationships governed by a fixed-duration contract of employment within the meaning of Article 1(1) of Council Directive 91/383/EEC of 25 June 1991 supplementing the measures to encourage improvements in the safety and health at work of workers with a fixed-duration employment relationship or a temporary employment relationship (*), or

(c) they are temporary employment relationships within the meaning of Article 1(2) of Directive 91/383/EEC, and the undertaking, business or part of the undertaking or business transferred is, or is part of, the temporary employment business which is the employer.

SECTION II
Safeguarding of employees' rights
Article 3

1. The transferor's rights and obligations arising from a contract of employment or from an employment relationship existing on the date of a transfer shall, by reason of such transfer, be transferred to the transferee.

Member States may provide that, after the date of transfer, the transferor and the transferee shall be jointly and severally liable in respect of obligations which arose before the date of transfer from a contract of employment or an employment relationship existing on the date of the transfer.

2. Member States may adopt appropriate measures to ensure that the transferor notifies the transferee of all the rights and obligations which

will be transferred to the transferee under this Article, so far as those rights and obligations are or ought to have been known to the transferor at the time of the transfer. A failure by the transferor to notify the transferee of any such right or obligation shall not affect the transfer of that right or obligation and the rights of any employees against the transferee and/or transferor in respect of that right or obligation.

3. Following the transfer, the transferee shall continue to observe the terms and conditions agreed in any collective agreement on the same terms applicable to the transferor under that agreement, until the date of termination or expiry of the collective agreement or the entry into force or application of another collective agreement.

    Member States may limit the period for observing such terms and conditions with the proviso that it shall not be less than one year.

4. (a) Unless Member States provide otherwise, paragraphs 1 and 3 shall not apply in relation to employees' rights to old-age, invalidity or survivors' benefits under supplementary company or inter-company pension schemes outside the statutory social security schemes in Member States.

    (b) Even where they do not provide in accordance with subparagraph (a) that paragraphs 1 and 3 apply in relation to such rights, Member States shall adopt the measures necessary to protect the interests of employees and of persons no longer employed in the transferor's business at the time of the transfer in respect of rights conferring on them immediate or prospective entitlement to old age benefits, including survivors' benefits, under supplementary schemes referred to in subparagraph (a).

Article 4

1. The transfer of the undertaking, business or part of the undertaking or business shall not in itself constitute grounds for dismissal by the transferor or the transferee. This provision shall not stand in the way of dismissals that may take place for economic, technical or organisational reasons entailing changes in the workforce.

    Member States may provide that the first subparagraph shall not apply to certain specific categories of employees who are not covered by the laws or practice of the Member States in respect of protection against dismissal.

2. If the contract of employment or the employment relationship is terminated because the transfer involves a substantial change in working conditions to the detriment of the employee, the employer shall be regarded as having been responsible for termination of the contract of employment or of the employment relationship.

Article 4a

1. Unless Member States provide otherwise, Articles 3 and 4 shall not apply to any transfer of an undertaking, business or part of an undertaking or business where the transferor is the subject of bankruptcy proceedings or any analogous insolvency proceedings which have been instituted with a view to the liquidation of the assets of the transferor and are under the supervision of a competent public authority (which may be an insolvency practitioner authorised by a competent public authority).

2. Where Articles 3 and 4 apply to a transfer during insolvency proceedings which have been opened in relation to a transferor (whether or not those proceedings have been instituted with a view to the liquidation of the assets of the transferor) and provided that such proceedings are under the supervision of a competent public authority (which may be an insolvency practitioner determined by national law) a Member State may provide that:

    (a) notwithstanding Article 3(1), the transferor's debts arising from any contracts of employment or employment relationships and payable before the transfer or before the opening of the insolvency proceedings shall not be transferred to the transferee, provided that such proceedings give rise, under the law of that Member State, to protection at least equivalent to that provided for in situations covered by Council Directive 80/987/EEC of 20 October 1980 on the approximation of the laws of the Member States relating to the protection of employees in the event of the insolvency of their employer (**);

    and, or alternatively, that

    (b) the transferee, transferor, or person or persons exercising the transferor's functions, on the one hand, and the representatives of the employees on the other hand may agree alterations, insofar as current law or practice permits, to the employees' terms and conditions of employment designed to safeguard employment opportunities by ensuring the survival of the undertaking, business or part of the undertaking or business.

3. A Member State may apply paragraph 2(b) to any transfers where the transferor is in a situation of serious economic crisis, as defined by national law, provided that the situation is declared by a competent public authority and open to judicial supervision, on condition that such provisions already exist in national law by 17 July 1998.

    The Commission shall present a report on the effects of this provision before 17 July 2003 and shall submit any appropriate proposals to the Council.

4. Member States shall take appropriate measures with a view to preventing misuse of insolvency proceedings in such a way as to deprive employees of the rights provided for in this Directive.

Article 5

1. If the undertaking, business or part of an undertaking or business preserves its autonomy, the status and function of the representatives or of the representation of the employees affected by the transfer shall be preserved on the same terms and subject to the same conditions as existed before the date of the transfer by virtue of law, regulation, administrative provision or agreement, provided that the conditions necessary for the constitution of the employees' representation are fulfilled.

    The first subparagraph shall not apply if, under the laws, regulations, administrative provisions or practice in the Member States, or by agreement with the representatives of the employees, the conditions necessary for the reappointment of the representatives of the employees or for the reconstitution of the representation of the employees are fulfilled.

    Where the transferor is the subject of bankruptcy proceedings or any analogous insolvency proceedings which have been instituted with a view to the liquidation of the assets of the transferor and are under the supervision of a competent public authority (which may be an insolvency practitioner authorised by a competent public authority), Member States may take the necessary measures to ensure that the transferred employees are properly represented until the new election or designation of representatives of the employees.

    If the undertaking, business or part of an undertaking or business does not preserve its autonomy, the Member States shall take the necessary measures to ensure that the employees transferred who were represented before the transfer continue to be properly represented during the period necessary for the reconstitution or reappointment of the representation of employees in accordance with national law or practice.

2. If the term of office of the representatives of the employees affected by the transfer expires as a result of the transfer, the representatives shall continue to enjoy the protection provided by the laws, regulations, administrative provisions or practice of the Member States.

SECTION III
Information and consultation
Article 6

1. The transferor and transferee shall be required to inform the representatives of their respective employees affected by the transfer of the following:
   - the date or proposed date of the transfer,
   - the reasons for the transfer,
   - the legal, economic and social implications of the transfer for the employees,
   - any measures envisaged in relation to the employees.

   The transferor must give such information to the representatives of his employees in good time before the transfer is carried out.

   The transferee must give such information to the representatives of his employees in good time, and in any event before his employees are directly affected by the transfer as regards their conditions of work and employment.

2. Where the transferor or the transferee envisages measures in relation to his employees, he shall consult the representatives of his employees in good time on such measures with a view to reaching an agreement.

3. Member States whose laws, regulations or administrative provisions provide that representatives of the employees may have recourse to an arbitration board to obtain a decision on the measures to be taken in relation to employees may limit the obligations laid down in paragraphs 1 and 2 to cases where the transfer carried out gives rise to a change in the business likely to entail serious disadvantages for a considerable number of the employees.

   The information and consultations shall cover at least the measures envisaged in relation to the employees.

The information must be provided and consultations taken place in good time before the change in the business as referred to in the first subparagraph is effected.

4.   The obligations laid down in this Article shall apply irrespective of whether the decision resulting in the transfer is taken by the employer or an undertaking controlling the employer.

In considering alleged breaches of the information and consultation requirements laid down by this Directive, the argument that such a breach occurred because the information was not provided by an undertaking controlling the employer shall not be accepted as an excuse.

5.   Member States may limit the obligations laid down in paragraphs 1, 2 and 3 to undertakings or businesses which, in terms of the number of employees, meet the conditions for the election or nomination of a collegiate body representing the employees.

6.   Member States shall provide that, where there are no representatives of the employees in an undertaking or business through no fault of their own, the employees concerned must be informed in advance of:
- the date or proposed date of the transfer,
- the reason for the transfer,
- the legal, economic and social implications of the transfer for the employees,
- any measures envisaged in relation to the employees.

SECTION IV

Final provisions
Article 7
This Directive shall not affect the right of Member States to apply or introduce laws, regulations or administrative provisions which are more favourable to employees or to promote or permit collective agreements or agreements between social partners more favourable to employees.

Article 7a
Member States shall introduce into their national legal systems such measures as are necessary to enable all employees and representatives of employees who consider themselves wronged by failure to comply with the obligations arising from this Directive to pursue their claims by judicial process after possible recourse to other competent authorities.

Article 7b

The Commission shall submit to the Council an analysis of the effects of the provisions of this Directive before 17 July 2006. It shall propose any amendment which may seem necessary.

(*) OJ L 206, 29. 7. 1991, p. 19.

(**) OJ L 283, 20. 10. 1980, p. 23. Directive as amended by Directive 87/164/EEC (OJ L 66, 11. 3. 1987, p. 11).'

Article 2

1   Member States shall bring into force the laws, regulations and administrative provisions necessary to comply with this Directive by 17 July 2001 at the latest or shall ensure that, by that date, at the latest, the employers' and employees' representatives have introduced the required provisions by means of agreement, Member States being obliged to take the necessary steps enabling them at all times to guarantee the results imposed by this Directive.

2   When Member States adopt the measures referred to in paragraph 1, they shall contain a reference to this Directive or shall be accompanied by such reference on the occasion on their official publication. The methods of making such reference shall be laid down by Member States.

Member States shall inform the Commission immediately of the measures they take to implement this Directive.

Article 3

This Directive shall enter into force on the day of its publication in the Official Journal of the European Communities.

Article 4

This Directive is addressed to the Member States.

Done at Luxembourg, 29 June 1998.

For the Council

The President

R. COOK

APPENDIX 2: TUPE REGULATIONS 2006

2006 No. 246

TERMS AND CONDITIONS OF EMPLOYMENT

The Transfer of Undertakings (Protection of Employment) Regulations 2006[1]

Made	*6th February 2006*
Laid before Parliament	*7th February 2006*
Coming into force	*6th April 2006*

The Secretary of State makes the following Regulations in exercise of the powers conferred upon him by section 2(2) of the European Communities Act 1972 (being a Minister designated for the purposes of that section in relation to rights and obligations relating to employers and employees on the transfer or merger of undertakings, businesses or parts of businesses) and section 38 of the Employment Relations Act 1999.

Citation, commencement and extent

1.(1) These Regulations may be cited as the Transfer of Undertakings (Protection of Employment) Regulations 2006.

(2) These Regulations shall come into force on 6 April 2006.

(3) These Regulations shall extend to Northern Ireland, except where otherwise provided.

Interpretation

2. (1) In these Regulations—

"assigned" means assigned other than on a temporary basis;

"collective agreement", "collective bargaining" and "trade union" have the same meanings respectively as in the 1992 Act;

"contract of employment" means any agreement between an employee and his employer determining the terms and conditions of his employment; references to "contractor" in regulation 3 shall include a sub-contractor;

"employee" means any individual who works for another person whether under a contract of service or apprenticeship or otherwise but

---

[1] As published. Note that new paragraph 13(2A) was introduced by Agency Workers Regulations 2010 (SI 2010/93), and that the 2014 TUPE Amendment Regulations paragraphs 5-11 introduce further amendments (see Appendix 3 below).

does not include anyone who provides services under a contract for services and references to a person's employer shall be construed accordingly;

"insolvency practitioner" has the meaning given to the expression by Part XIII of the Insolvency Act 1986; references to "organised grouping of employees" shall include a single employee;

"recognised" has the meaning given to the expression by section 178(3) of the 1992 Act;

"relevant transfer" means a transfer or a service provision change to which these Regulations apply in accordance with regulation 3 and "transferor" and "transferee" shall be construed accordingly and in the case of a service provision change falling within regulation 3(1)(b), "the transferor" means the person who carried out the activities prior to the service provision change and "the transferee" means the person who carries out the activities as a result of the service provision change;

"the 1992 Act" means the Trade Union and Labour Relations (Consolidation) Act 1992;

"the 1996 Act" means the Employment Rights Act 1996; "the 1996 Tribunals Act" means the Employment Tribunals Act 1996;

"the 1981 Regulations" means the Transfer of Undertakings (Protection of Employment) Regulations 1981.

(2) For the purposes of these Regulations the representative of a trade union recognised by an employer is an official or other person authorised to carry on collective bargaining with that employer by that trade union.

(3) In the application of these Regulations to Northern Ireland the Regulations shall have effect as set out in Schedule 1.

A relevant transfer

3. (1) These Regulations apply to—

    (a) a transfer of an undertaking, business or part of an undertaking or business situated immediately before the transfer in the United Kingdom to another person where there is a transfer of an economic entity which retains its identity;

    (b) a service provision change, that is a situation in which—

        (i) activities cease to be carried out by a person ("a client") on his own behalf and are carried out instead by another person on the client's behalf ("a contractor");

(ii) activities cease to be carried out by a contractor on a client's behalf (whether or not those activities had previously been carried out by the client on his own behalf) and are carried out instead by another person ("a subsequent contractor") on the client's behalf; or

(iii) activities cease to be carried out by a contractor or a subsequent contractor on a client's behalf (whether or not those activities had previously been carried out by the client on his own behalf) and are carried out instead by the client on his own behalf, and in which the conditions set out in paragraph (3) are satisfied.

(2) In this regulation "economic entity" means an organised grouping of resources which has the objective of pursuing an economic activity, whether or not that activity is central or ancillary.

(3) The conditions referred to in paragraph (1)(b) are that—
   (a) immediately before the service provision change—
      (i) there is an organised grouping of employees situated in Great Britain which has as its principal purpose the carrying out of the activities concerned on behalf of the client;
      (ii) the client intends that the activities will, following the service provision change, be carried out by the transferee other than in connection with a single specific event or task of short-term duration; and
   (b) the activities concerned do not consist wholly or mainly of the supply of goods for the client's use.

(4) Subject to paragraph (1), these Regulations apply to—
   (a) public and private undertakings engaged in economic activities whether or not they are operating for gain;
   (b) a transfer or service provision change howsoever effected notwithstanding—
      (i) that the transfer of an undertaking, business or part of an undertaking or business is governed or effected by the law of a country or territory outside the United Kingdom or that the service provision change is governed or effected by the law of a country or territory outside Great Britain;
      (ii) that the employment of persons employed in the undertaking, business or part transferred or, in the case of a service provision change, persons employed in the organised grouping of employees, is governed by any such law;

(c) a transfer of an undertaking, business or part of an undertaking or business (which may also be a service provision change) where persons employed in the undertaking, business or part transferred ordinarily work outside the United Kingdom.

(5) An administrative reorganisation of public administrative authorities or the transfer of administrative functions between public administrative authorities is not a relevant transfer.

(6) A relevant transfer —
   (a) may be effected by a series of two or more transactions; and
   (b) may take place whether or not any property is transferred to the transferee by the transferor.

(7) Where, in consequence (whether directly or indirectly) of the transfer of an undertaking, business or part of an undertaking or business which was situated immediately before the transfer in the United Kingdom, a ship within the meaning of the Merchant Shipping Act 1995 registered in the United Kingdom ceases to be so registered, these Regulations shall not affect the right conferred by section 29 of that Act (right of seamen to be discharged when ship ceases to be registered in the United Kingdom) on a seaman employed in the ship.

Effect of relevant transfer on contracts of employment
4. (1) Except where objection is made under paragraph (7), a relevant transfer shall not operate so as to terminate the contract of employment of any person employed by the transferor and assigned to the organised grouping of resources or employees that is subject to the relevant transfer, which would otherwise be terminated by the transfer, but any such contract shall have effect after the transfer as if originally made between the person so employed and the transferee.

(2) Without prejudice to paragraph (1), but subject to paragraph (6), and regulations 8 and 15(9), on the completion of a relevant transfer —
   (a) all the transferor's rights, powers, duties and liabilities under or in connection with any such contract shall be transferred by virtue of this regulation to the transferee; and
   (b) any act or omission before the transfer is completed, of or in relation to the transferor in respect of that contract or a person assigned to that organised grouping of resources or employees, shall be deemed to have been an act or omission of or in relation to the transferee.

(3) Any reference in paragraph (1) to a person employed by the transferor and assigned to the organised grouping of resources or employees that is subject to a relevant transfer, is a reference to a person so employed immediately before the transfer, or who would have been so employed if he had not been dismissed in the circumstances described in regulation 7(1), including, where the transfer is effected by a series of two or more transactions, a person so employed and assigned or who would have been so employed and assigned immediately before any of those transactions.

(4) Subject to regulation 9, in respect of a contract of employment that is, or will be, transferred by paragraph (1), any purported variation of the contract shall be void if the sole or principal reason for the variation is—

    (a) the transfer itself; or

    (b) a reason connected with the transfer that is not an economic, technical or organisational reason entailing changes in the workforce.

(5) Paragraph (4) shall not prevent the employer and his employee, whose contract of employment is, or will be, transferred by paragraph (1), from agreeing a variation of that contract if the sole or principal reason for the variation is—

    (a) a reason connected with the transfer that is an economic, technical or organisational reason entailing changes in the workforce; or

    (b) a reason unconnected with the transfer.

(6) Paragraph (2) shall not transfer or otherwise affect the liability of any person to be prosecuted for, convicted of and sentenced for any offence.

(7) Paragraphs (1) and (2) shall not operate to transfer the contract of employment and the rights, powers, duties and liabilities under or in connection with it of an employee who informs the transferor or the transferee that he objects to becoming employed by the transferee.

(8) Subject to paragraphs (9) and (11), where an employee so objects, the relevant transfer shall operate so as to terminate his contract of employment with the transferor but he shall not be treated, for any purpose, as having been dismissed by the transferor.

(9) Subject to regulation 9, where a relevant transfer involves or would involve a substantial change in working conditions to the material detriment of a person whose contract of employment is or would be

transferred under paragraph (1), such an employee may treat the contract of employment as having been terminated, and the employee shall be treated for any purpose as having been dismissed by the employer.

(10) No damages shall be payable by an employer as a result of a dismissal falling within paragraph (9) in respect of any failure by the employer to pay wages to an employee in respect of a notice period which the employee has failed to work.

(11) Paragraphs (1), (7), (8) and (9) are without prejudice to any right of an employee arising apart from these Regulations to terminate his contract of employment without notice in acceptance of a repudiatory breach of contract by his employer.

Effect of relevant transfer on collective agreements

5. Where at the time of a relevant transfer there exists a collective agreement made by or on behalf of the transferor with a trade union recognised by the transferor in respect of any employee whose contract of employment is preserved by regulation 4(1) above, then—

    (a) without prejudice to sections 179 and 180 of the 1992 Act (collective agreements presumed to be unenforceable in specified circumstances) that agreement, in its application in relation to the employee, shall, after the transfer, have effect as if made by or on behalf of the transferee with that trade union, and accordingly anything done under or in connection with it, in its application in relation to the employee, by or in relation to the transferor before the transfer, shall, after the transfer, be deemed to have been done by or in relation to the transferee; and

    (b) any order made in respect of that agreement, in its application in relation to the employee, shall, after the transfer, have effect as if the transferee were a party to the agreement.

Effect of relevant transfer on trade union recognition

6. (1) This regulation applies where after a relevant transfer the transferred organised grouping of resources or employees maintains an identity distinct from the remainder of the transferee's undertaking.

(2) Where before such a transfer an independent trade union is recognised to any extent by the transferor in respect of employees of any description who in consequence of the transfer become employees of the transferee, then, after the transfer—

(a) the trade union shall be deemed to have been recognised by the transferee to the same extent in respect of employees of that description so employed; and

(b) any agreement for recognition may be varied or rescinded accordingly.

Dismissal of employee because of relevant transfer

7. (1) Where either before or after a relevant transfer, any employee of the transferor or transferee is dismissed, that employee shall be treated for the purposes of Part X of the 1996 Act (unfair dismissal) as unfairly dismissed if the sole or principal reason for his dismissal is—

(a) the transfer itself; or

(b) a reason connected with the transfer that is not an economic, technical or organisational reason entailing changes in the workforce.

(2) This paragraph applies where the sole or principal reason for the dismissal is a reason connected with the transfer that is an economic, technical or organisational reason entailing changes in the workforce of either the transferor or the transferee before or after a relevant transfer.

(3) Where paragraph (2) applies—

(a) paragraph (1) shall not apply;

(b) without prejudice to the application of section 98(4) of the 1996 Act (test of fair dismissal), the dismissal shall, for the purposes of sections 98(1) and 135 of that Act (reason for dismissal), be regarded as having been for redundancy where section 98(2)(c) of that Act applies, or otherwise for a substantial reason of a kind such as to justify the dismissal of an employee holding the position which that employee held.

(4) The provisions of this regulation apply irrespective of whether the employee in question is assigned to the organised grouping of resources or employees that is, or will be, transferred.

(5) Paragraph (1) shall not apply in relation to the dismissal of any employee which was required by reason of the application of section 5 of the Aliens Restriction (Amendment) Act 1919 to his employment.

(6) Paragraph (1) shall not apply in relation to a dismissal of an employee if the application of section 94 of the 1996 Act to the dismissal of the employee is excluded by or under any provision of the 1996 Act, the 1996 Tribunals Act or the 1992 Act.

Insolvency

8.(1) If at the time of a relevant transfer the transferor is subject to relevant insolvency proceedings paragraphs (2) to (6) apply.

(2) In this regulation "relevant employee" means an employee of the transferor—

    (a) whose contract of employment transfers to the transferee by virtue of the operation of these Regulations; or

    (b) whose employment with the transferor is terminated before the time of the relevant transfer in the circumstances described in regulation 7(1).

(3) The relevant statutory scheme specified in paragraph (4)(b) (including that sub-paragraph as applied by paragraph 5 of Schedule 1) shall apply in the case of a relevant employee irrespective of the fact that the qualifying requirement that the employee's employment has been terminated is not met and for those purposes the date of the transfer shall be treated as the date of the termination and the transferor shall be treated as the employer.

(4) In this regulation the "relevant statutory schemes" are—

    (a) Chapter VI of Part XI of the 1996 Act;

    (b) Part XII of the 1996 Act.

(5) Regulation 4 shall not operate to transfer liability for the sums payable to the relevant employee under the relevant statutory schemes.

(6) In this regulation "relevant insolvency proceedings" means insolvency proceedings which have been opened in relation to the transferor not with a view to the liquidation of the assets of the transferor and which are under the supervision of an insolvency practitioner.

(7) Regulations 4 and 7 do not apply to any relevant transfer where the transferor is the subject of bankruptcy proceedings or any analogous insolvency proceedings which have been instituted with a view to the liquidation of the assets of the transferor and are under the supervision of an insolvency practitioner.

Variations of contract where transferors are subject to relevant insolvency proceedings

9. (1) If at the time of a relevant transfer the transferor is subject to relevant insolvency proceedings these Regulations shall not prevent the transferor or transferee (or an insolvency practitioner) and appropriate representatives of assigned employees agreeing to permitted variations.

(2) For the purposes of this regulation "appropriate representatives" are—

(a) if the employees are of a description in respect of which an independent trade union is recognised by their employer, representatives of the trade union; or

(b) in any other case, whichever of the following employee representatives the employer chooses—

   (i) employee representatives appointed or elected by the assigned employees (whether they make the appointment or election alone or with others) otherwise than for the purposes of this regulation, who (having regard to the purposes for, and the method by which they were appointed or elected) have authority from those employees to agree permitted variations to contracts of employment on their behalf;

   (ii) employee representatives elected by assigned employees (whether they make the appointment or election alone or with others) for these particular purposes, in an election satisfying requirements identical to those contained in regulation 14 except those in regulation 14(1)(d).

(3) An individual may be an appropriate representative for the purposes of both this regulation and regulation 13 provided that where the representative is not a trade union representative he is either elected by or has authority from assigned employees (within the meaning of this regulation) and affected employees (as described in regulation 13(1)).

(4) In section 168 of the 1992 Act (time off for carrying out trade union duties) in subsection (1), after paragraph (c) there is inserted—

" , or

(d) negotiations with a view to entering into an agreement under regulation 9 of the Transfer of Undertakings (Protection of Employment) Regulations 2006 that applies to employees of the employer, or

(e) the performance on behalf of employees of the employer of functions related to or connected with the making of an agreement under that regulation.".

(5) Where assigned employees are represented by non-trade union representatives—

 (a) the agreement recording a permitted variation must be in writing and signed by each of the representatives who have made it or, where that is not reasonably practicable, by a duly authorised agent of that representative; and

    (b) the employer must, before the agreement is made available for signature, provide all employees to whom it is intended to apply on the date on which it is to come into effect with copies of the text of the agreement and such guidance as those employees might reasonably require in order to understand it fully.

(6) A permitted variation shall take effect as a term or condition of the assigned employee's contract of employment in place, where relevant, of any term or condition which it varies.

(7) In this regulation— "assigned employees" means those employees assigned to the organised grouping of resources or employees that is the subject of a relevant transfer;

"permitted variation" is a variation to the contract of employment of an assigned employee where—

    (a) the sole or principal reason for it is the transfer itself or a reason connected with the transfer that is not an economic, technical or organisational reason entailing changes in the workforce; and

    (b) it is designed to safeguard employment opportunities by ensuring the survival of the undertaking, business or part of the undertaking or business that is the subject of the relevant transfer;

"relevant insolvency proceedings" has the meaning given to the expression by regulation 8(6).

Pensions

10. (1) Regulations 4 and 5 shall not apply—

    (a) to so much of a contract of employment or collective agreement as relates to an occupational pension scheme within the meaning of the Pension Schemes Act 1993; or

    (b) to any rights, powers, duties or liabilities under or in connection with any such contract or subsisting by virtue of any such agreement and relating to such a scheme or otherwise arising in connection with that person's employment and relating to such a scheme.

(2) For the purposes of paragraphs (1) and (3), any provisions of an occupational pension scheme which do not relate to benefits for old age, invalidity or survivors shall not be treated as being part of the scheme.

(3) An employee whose contract of employment is transferred in the circumstances described in regulation 4(1) shall not be entitled to bring a claim against the transferor for—

    (a) breach of contract; or

(b) constructive unfair dismissal under section 95(1)(c) of the 1996 Act, arising out of a loss or reduction in his rights under an occupational pension scheme in consequence of the transfer, save insofar as the alleged breach of contract or dismissal (as the case may be) occurred prior to the date on which these Regulations took effect.

Notification of Employee Liability Information

11. (1) The transferor shall notify to the transferee the employee liability information of any person employed by him who is assigned to the organised grouping of resources or employees that is the subject of a relevant transfer —

(a) in writing; or

(b) by making it available to him in a readily accessible form.

(2) In this regulation and in regulation 12 "employee liability information" means—

(a) the identity and age of the employee;

(b) those particulars of employment that an employer is obliged to give to an employee under section 1 of the 1996 Act;

(c) information of any—

(i) disciplinary procedure taken against an employee;

(ii) grievance procedure taken by an employee, within the previous two years, in circumstances where the Employment Act 2002 (Dispute Resolution) Regulations 2004 apply;

(d) information of any court or tribunal case, claim or action—

(i) brought by an employee against the transferor, within the previous two years;

(ii) that the transferor has reasonable grounds to believe that an employee may bring against the transferee, arising out of the employee's employment with the transferor; and

(e) information of any collective agreement which will have effect after the transfer, in its application in relation to the employee, under regulation 5(a).

(3) Employee liability information shall contain information as at a specified date not more than fourteen days before the date on which the information is notified to the transferee.

(4) The duty to provide employee liability information in paragraph (1) shall include a duty to provide employee liability information of any person who would have been employed by the transferor and assigned to the organised grouping of resources or employees that is

the subject of a relevant transfer immediately before the transfer if he had not been dismissed in the circumstances described in regulation 7(1), including, where the transfer is effected by a series of two or more transactions, a person so employed and assigned or who would have been so employed and assigned immediately before any of those transactions.

(5) Following notification of the employee liability information in accordance with this regulation, the transferor shall notify the transferee in writing of any change in the employee liability information.

(6) A notification under this regulation shall be given not less than fourteen days before the relevant transfer or, if special circumstances make this not reasonably practicable, as soon as reasonably practicable thereafter.

(7) A notification under this regulation may be given—
    (a) in more than one instalment;
    (b) indirectly, through a third party.

Remedy for failure to notify employee liability information
12. (1) On or after a relevant transfer, the transferee may present a complaint to an employment tribunal that the transferor has failed to comply with any provision of regulation 11.

(2) An employment tribunal shall not consider a complaint under this regulation unless it is presented—
    (a) before the end of the period of three months beginning with the date of the relevant transfer;
    (b) within such further period as the tribunal considers reasonable in a case where it is satisfied that it was not reasonably practicable for the complaint to be presented before the end of that period of three months.

(3) Where an employment tribunal finds a complaint under paragraph (1) well-founded, the tribunal—
    (a) shall make a declaration to that effect; and
    (b) may make an award of compensation to be paid by the transferor to the transferee.

(4) The amount of the compensation shall be such as the tribunal considers just and equitable in all the circumstances, subject to paragraph (5), having particular regard to—

(a) any loss sustained by the transferee which is attributable to the matters complained of; and

(b) the terms of any contract between the transferor and the transferee relating to the transfer under which the transferor may be liable to pay any sum to the transferee in respect of a failure to notify the transferee of employee liability information.

(5) Subject to paragraph (6), the amount of compensation awarded under paragraph (3) shall be not less than £500 per employee in respect of whom the transferor has failed to comply with a provision of regulation 11, unless the tribunal considers it just and equitable, in all the circumstances, to award a lesser sum.

(6) In ascertaining the loss referred to in paragraph (4)(a) the tribunal shall apply the same rule concerning the duty of a person to mitigate his loss as applies to any damages recoverable under the common law of England and Wales, Northern Ireland or Scotland, as applicable.

(7) Section 18 of the 1996 Tribunals Act (conciliation) shall apply to the right conferred by this regulation and to proceedings under this regulation as it applies to the rights conferred by that Act and the employment tribunal proceedings mentioned in that Act.

Duty to inform and consult representatives

13. (1) In this regulation and regulations 14 and 15 references to affected employees, in relation to a relevant transfer, are to any employees of the transferor or the transferee (whether or not assigned to the organised grouping of resources or employees that is the subject of a relevant transfer) who may be affected by the transfer or may be affected by measures taken in connection with it; and references to the employer shall be construed accordingly.

(2) Long enough before a relevant transfer to enable the employer of any affected employees to consult the appropriate representatives of any affected employees, the employer shall inform those representatives of—

(a) the fact that the transfer is to take place, the date or proposed date of the transfer and the reasons for it;

(b) the legal, economic and social implications of the transfer for any affected employees;

(c) the measures which he envisages he will, in connection with the transfer, take in relation to any affected employees or, if he envisages that no measures will be so taken, that fact; and

(d) if the employer is the transferor, the measures, in connection with the transfer, which he envisages the transferee will take in relation to any affected employees who will become employees of the transferee after the transfer by virtue of regulation 4 or, if he envisages that no measures will be so taken, that fact.

(2A) Where information is to be supplied under paragraph (2) by an employer—

(a) this must include suitable information relating to the use of agency workers (if any) by that employer; and

(b) "suitable information relating to the use of agency workers" means—

(i) the number of agency workers working temporarily for and under the supervision and direction of the employer;

(ii) the parts of the employer's undertaking in which those agency workers are working; and

(iii) the type of work those agency workers are carrying out.

(3) For the purposes of this regulation the appropriate representatives of any affected employees are—

(a) if the employees are of a description in respect of whichan independent trade union is recognised by their employer, representatives of the trade union; or

(b) in any other case, whichever of the following employee representatives the employer chooses—

(4) The transferee shall give the transferor such information at such a time as will enable the transferor to perform the duty imposed on him by virtue of paragraph (2)(d).

(5) The information which is to be given to the appropriate representatives shall be given to each of them by being delivered to them, or sent by post to an address notified by them to the employer, or (in the case of representatives of a trade union) sent by post to the trade union at the address of its head or main office.

(6) An employer of an affected employee who envisages that he will take measures in relation to an affected employee, in connection with the relevant transfer, shall consult the appropriate representatives of that employee with a view to seeking their agreement to the intended measures.

(7) In the course of those consultations the employer shall—

    (a) consider any representations made by the appropriate representatives; and

    (b) reply to those representations and, if he rejects any of those representations, state his reasons.

(8) The employer shall allow the appropriate representatives access to any affected employees and shall afford to those representatives such accommodation and other facilities as may be appropriate.

(9) If in any case there are special circumstances which render it not reasonably practicable for an employer to perform a duty imposed on him by any of paragraphs (2) to (7), he shall take all such steps towards performing that duty as are reasonably practicable in the circumstances.

(10) Where—

    (a) the employer has invited any of the affected employee to elect employee representatives; and

    (b) the invitation was issued long enough before the time when the employer is required to give information under paragraph (2) to allow them to elect representatives by that time,

    (c) the employer shall be treated as complying with the requirements of this regulation in relation to those employees if he complies with those requirements as soon as is reasonably practicable after the election of the representatives.

(11) If, after the employer has invited any affected employees to elect representatives, they fail to do so within a reasonable time, he shall give to any affected employees the information set out in paragraph (2).

(12) The duties imposed on an employer by this regulation shall apply irrespective of whether the decision resulting in the relevant transfer is taken by the employer or a person controlling the employer.

Election of employee representatives

14. (1) The requirements for the election of employee representatives under regulation 13(3) are that—

    (a) the employer shall make such arrangements as are reasonably practicable to ensure that the election is fair;

    (b) the employer shall determine the number of representatives to be elected so that there are sufficient representatives to represent the interests of all affected employees having regard to the number and classes of those employees;

(c) the employer shall determine whether the affected employees should be represented either by representatives of all the affected employees or by representatives of particular classes of those employees;

(d) before the election the employer shall determine the term of office as employee representatives so that it is of sufficient length to enable information to be given and consultations under regulation 13 to be completed;

(e) the candidates for election as employee representatives are affected employees on the date of the election;

(f) no affected employee is unreasonably excluded from standing for election;

(g) all affected employees on the date of the election are entitled to vote for employee representatives;

(h) the employees entitled to vote may vote for as many candidates as there are representatives to be elected to represent them or, if there are to be representatives for particular classes of employees, may vote for as many candidates as there are representatives to be elected to represent their particular class of employee;

(i) the election is conducted so as to secure that—

    (i) so far as is reasonably practicable, those voting do so in secret; and

    (ii) the votes given at the election are accurately counted.

(2) Where, after an election of employee representatives satisfying the requirements of paragraph (1) has been held, one of those elected ceases to act as an employee representative and as a result any affected employees are no longer represented, those employees shall elect another representative by an election satisfying the requirements of paragraph (1)(a), (e), (f) and (i).

Failure to inform or consult

15. (1) Where an employer has failed to comply with a requirement of regulation 13 or regulation 14, a complaint may be presented to an employment tribunal on that ground—

(a) in the case of a failure relating to the election of employee representatives, by any of his employees who are affected employees;

(b) in the case of any other failure relating to employee representatives, by any of the employee representatives to whom the failure related;

(c) in the case of failure relating to representatives of a trade union, by the trade union; and

(d) in any other case, by any of his employees who are affected employees.

(2) If on a complaint under paragraph (1) a question arises whether or not it was reasonably practicable for an employer to perform a particular duty or as to what steps he took towards performing it, it shall be for him to show—

(a) that there were special circumstances which rendered it not reasonably practicable for him to perform the duty; and

(b) that he took all such steps towards its performance as were reasonably practicable in those circumstances.

(3) If on a complaint under paragraph (1) a question arises as to whether or not an employee representative was an appropriate representative for the purposes of regulation 13, it shall be for the employer to show that the employee representative had the necessary authority to represent the affected employees.

(4) On a complaint under paragraph (1)(a) it shall be for the employer to show that the requirements in regulation 14 have been satisfied.

(5) On a complaint against a transferor that he had failed to perform the duty imposed upon him by virtue of regulation 13(2)(d) or, so far as relating thereto, regulation 13(9), he may not show that it was not reasonably practicable for him to perform the duty in question for the reason that the transferee had failed to give him the requisite information at the requisite time in accordance with regulation 13(4) unless he gives the transferee notice of his intention to show that fact; and the giving of the notice shall make the transferee a party to the proceedings.

(6) In relation to any complaint under paragraph (1), a failure on the part of a person controlling (directly or indirectly) the employer to provide information to the employer shall not constitute special circumstances rendering it not reasonably practicable for the employer to comply with such a requirement.

(7) Where the tribunal finds a complaint against a transferee under paragraph (1) well-founded it shall make a declaration to that effect and may order the transferee to pay appropriate compensation to such descriptions of affected employees as may be specified in the award.

(8) Where the tribunal finds a complaint against a transferor under paragraph (1) well-founded it shall make a declaration to that effect and may—

    (a) order the transferor, subject to paragraph (9), to pay appropriate compensation to such descriptions of affected employees as may be specified in the award; or

    (b) if the complaint is that the transferor did not perform the duty mentioned in paragraph (5) and the transferor (after giving due notice) shows the facts so mentioned, order the transferee to pay appropriate compensation to such descriptions of affected employees as may be specified in the award.

(9) The transferee shall be jointly and severally liable with the transferor in respect of compensation payable under sub-paragraph (8)(a) or paragraph (11).

(10) An employee may present a complaint to an employment tribunal on the ground that he is an employee of a description to which an order under paragraph (7) or (8) relates and that—

    (a) in respect of an order under paragraph (7), the transferee has failed, wholly or in part, to pay him compensation in pursuance of the order;

    (b) in respect of an order under paragraph (8), the transferor or transferee, as applicable, has failed, wholly or in part, to pay him compensation in pursuance of the order.

(11) Where the tribunal finds a complaint under paragraph (10) well-founded it shall order the transferor or transferee as applicable to pay the complainant the amount of compensation which it finds is due to him.

(12) An employment tribunal shall not consider a complaint under paragraph (1) or (10) unless it is presented to the tribunal before the end of the period of three months beginning with—

    (a) in respect of a complaint under paragraph (1), the date on which the relevant transfer is completed; or

    (b) in respect of a complaint under paragraph (10), the date of the tribunal's order under paragraph (7) or (8), or within such further period as the tribunal considers reasonable in a case where it is satisfied that it was not reasonably practicable for the complaint to be presented before the end of the period of three months.

Failure to inform or consult: supplemental

16. (1) Section 205(1) of the 1996 Act (complaint to be sole remedy for breach of relevant rights) and section 18 of the 1996 Tribunals Act (conciliation) shall apply to the rights conferred by regulation 15 and to proceedings under this regulation as they apply to the rights conferred by those Acts and the employment tribunal proceedings mentioned in those Acts.

(2) An appeal shall lie and shall lie only to the Employment Appeal Tribunal on a question of law arising from any decision of, or arising in any proceedings before, an employment tribunal under or by virtue of these Regulations; and section 11(1) of the Tribunals and Inquiries Act 1992 (appeals from certain tribunals to the High Court) shall not apply in relation to any such proceedings.

(3) "Appropriate compensation" in regulation 15 means such sum not exceeding thirteen weeks' pay for the employee in question as the tribunal considers just and equitable having regard to the seriousness of the failure of the employer to comply with his duty.

(4) Sections 220 to 228 of the 1996 Act shall apply for calculating the amount of a week's pay for any employee for the purposes of paragraph (3) and, for the purposes of that calculation, the calculation date shall be—

(a) in the case of an employee who is dismissed by reason of redundancy (within the meaning of sections 139 and 155 of the 1996 Act) the date which is the calculation date for the purposes of any entitlement of his to a redundancy payment (within the meaning of those sections) or which would be that calculation date if he were so entitled;

(b) in the case of an employee who is dismissed for any other reason, the effective date of termination (within the meaning of sections 95(1) and (2) and 97 of the 1996 Act) of his contract of employment;

(c) in any other case, the date of the relevant transfer.

Employers' Liability Compulsory Insurance

17. (1) Paragraph (2) applies where—

(a) by virtue of section 3(1)(a) or (b) of the Employers' Liability (Compulsory Insurance) Act 1969 ("the 1969 Act"), the transferor is not required by that Act to effect any insurance; or

(b) by virtue of section 3(1)(c) of the 1969 Act, the transferor is exempted from the requirement of that Act to effect insurance.

(2) Where this paragraph applies, on completion of a relevant transfer the transferor and the transferee shall be jointly and severally liable in respect of any liability referred to in section 1(1) of the 1969 Act, in so far as such liability relates to the employee's employment with the transferor.

Restriction on contracting out

18. Section 203 of the 1996 Act (restrictions on contracting out) shall apply in relation to these Regulations as if they were contained in that Act, save for that section shall not apply in so far as these Regulations provide for an agreement (whether a contract of employment or not) to exclude or limit the operation of these Regulations.

Amendment to the 1996 Act

19. In section 104 of the 1996 Act (assertion of statutory right) in subsection (4)—

    (a) the word "and" at the end of paragraph (c) is omitted; and

    (b) after paragraph (d), there is inserted—

    " , and

       (e) the rights conferred by the Transfer of Undertakings (Protection of Employment) Regulations 2006.".

Repeals, revocations and amendments

20. (1) Subject to regulation 21, the 1981 Regulations are revoked.

(2) Section 33 of, and paragraph 4 of Schedule 9 to, the Trade Union Reform and Employment Rights Act 1993 are repealed.

(3) Schedule 2 (consequential amendments) shall have effect.

Transitional provisions and savings

21. (1) These Regulations shall apply in relation to—

    (a) a relevant transfer that takes place on or after 6 April 2006;

    (b) a transfer or service provision change, not falling within sub-paragraph (a), that takes place on or after 6 April 2006 and is regarded by virtue of any enactment as a relevant transfer.

(2) The 1981 Regulations shall continue to apply in relation to—

    (a) a relevant transfer (within the meaning of the 1981 Regulations) that took place before 6 April 2006;

    (b) a transfer, not falling within sub-paragraph (a), that took place before 6 April 2006 and is regarded by virtue of any enactment as a relevant transfer (within the meaning of the 1981 Regulations).

(3) In respect of a relevant transfer that takes place on or after 6 April 2006, any action taken by a transferor or transferee to discharge a duty that applied to them under regulation 10 or 10A of the 1981 Regulations shall be deemed to satisfy the corresponding obligation imposed by regulations 13 and 14 of these Regulations, insofar as that action would have discharged those obligations had the action taken place on or after 6 April 2006.

(4) The duty on a transferor to provide a transferee with employee liability information shall not apply in the case of a relevant transfer that takes place on or before 19 April 2006.

(5) Regulations 13, 14, 15 and 16 shall not apply in the case of a service provision change that is not also a transfer of an undertaking, business or part of an undertaking or business that takes place on or before 4 May 2006.

(6) The repeal of paragraph 4 of Schedule 9 to the Trade Union Reform and Employment Rights Act 1993 does not affect the continued operation of that paragraph so far as it remains capable of having effect.

Gerry Sutcliffe
Parliamentary Under Secretary of State for Employment Relations and Consumer Affairs Department of Trade and Industry

6th February 2006

APPENDIX 3: TUPE AMENDMENT REGULATIONS 2014

2014 No. 16

TERMS AND CONDITIONS OF EMPLOYMENT

The Collective Redundancies and Transfer of Undertakings (Protection of Employment) (Amendment) Regulations 2014

Made - - - -	*8th January 2014*
Laid before Parliament	*10th January 2014*
Coming into force - -	*31st January 2014*

The Secretary of State makes these Regulations in exercise of the powers conferred by section 2(2) of the European Communities Act 1972 and section 38 of the Employment Relations Act 1999.

The Secretary of State is a Minister designated for the purposes of section 2(2) of the European Communities Act 1972 in relation to measures relating to dismissals or terminations of employment contracts where such dismissals or terminations are effected by an employer for one or more reasons not related to the individual workers concerned and in relation to rights and obligations relating to employers and employees on the transfer or merger of undertakings, businesses or parts of businesses.

Citation, commencement and extent

1.—(1) These Regulations may be cited as the Collective Redundancies and Transfer of Undertakings (Protection of Employment) (Amendment) Regulations 2014.

(2) These Regulations come into force on 31st January 2014.

(3) These Regulations do not extend to Northern Ireland.

Interpretation

2. For the purposes of these Regulations—

"TUPE transfer" means—

    (a) a relevant transfer under the Transfer of Undertakings (Protection of Employment) Regulations 2006, or

    (b) anything else regarded, by virtue of an enactment, as a relevant transfer for the purposes of those Regulations.

Amendment of the Trade Union and Labour Relations (Consolidation) Act 1992

3.—(1) In Chapter 2 of Part 4 of the Trade Union and Labour Relations (Consolidation) Act 1992 (industrial relations: procedure for handling redundancies), after section 198 insert—

"**Employees being transferred to the employer from another undertaking**
198A.—(1) This section applies where the following conditions are met—

(a) there is to be, or is likely to be, a relevant transfer,

(b) the transferee is proposing to dismiss as redundant 20 or more
employees at one establishment within a period of 90 days or less,
and (c) the individuals who work for the transferor and who are to
be (or are likely to be) transferred to the transferee's employment
under the transfer ("transferring individuals") include one or more
individuals who may be affected by the proposed dismissals or by
measures taken in connection with the proposed dismissals.

(2) Where this section applies, the transferee may elect to consult, or to start
to consult, representatives of affected transferring individuals about the
proposed dismissals before the transfer takes place ("pre-transfer
consultation").

(3) Any such election—

(a) may be made only if the transferor agrees to it, and

(b) must be made by way of written notice to the transferor.

(4) If the transferee elects to carry out pre-transfer consultation—

(a) sections 188 to 198 apply from the time of the election (and
continue to apply after the transfer) as if the transferee were
already the transferring individuals' employer and as if any
transferring individuals who may be affected by the proposed
dismissals were already employed at the establishment mentioned
in subsection (1)(b) (but this is subject to section 198B), and

(b) the transferor may provide information or other assistance to the
transferee to help the transferee meet the requirements of this
Chapter.

(5) A transferee who elects to carry out pre-transfer consultation may
cancel that election at any time by written notice to the transferor.

(6) If the transferee cancels an election to carry out pre-transfer
consultation—

(a) sections 188 to 198 no longer apply as mentioned in subsection
(4)(a),

(b) anything done under those sections has no effect so far as it was
done in reliance on the election,

(c) if the transferee notified an appropriate representative, a
transferring individual or the Secretary of State of the election or

the proposed dismissals, the transferee must notify him or her of the cancellation as soon as reasonably practicable, and

(d) the transferee may not make another election under subsection (2) in relation to the proposed dismissals.

(7) For the purposes of this section and section 198B—

"affected transferring individual" means a transferring individual who may be affected by the proposed dismissals or who may be affected by measures taken in connection with the proposed dismissals;

"pre-transfer consultation" has the meaning given in subsection (2);

"relevant transfer" means—

(a) a relevant transfer under the Transfer of Undertakings (Protection of Employment) Regulations 2006,

(b) anything else regarded, by virtue of an enactment, as a relevant transfer for the purposes of those Regulations, or

(c) where an enactment provides a power to make provision which is the same as or similar to those Regulations, any other novation of a contract of employment effected in the exercise of that power,

and "transferor" and "transferee" are to be construed accordingly;

"transferring individual" has the meaning given in subsection (1)(c).

Section 198A: supplementary

198B.—(1) Where section 198A applies and the transferee elects to carry out pre-transfer consultation (and has not cancelled the election), the application under section 198A(4)(a) of sections 188 to 198 is (both before and after the transfer) subject to the following modifications—

(a) for section 188(1B)(a) substitute—

"(a) for transferring individuals of a description in respect of which an independent trade union is recognised by the transferor, representatives of that trade union,

(aa) for employees, other than transferring individuals, of a description in respect of which an independent trade union is recognised by the transferee, representatives of that trade union, or";

(b) in section 188(5), for "the employer" substitute "the transferor or transferee";

(c) in section 188(5A), for "shall allow the appropriate representatives access to the affected employees and shall afford to those representatives such accommodation and other facilities as may be appropriate" substitute "shall ensure that the appropriate representatives are allowed access to the affected transferring individuals and that such accommodation and other facilities as may be appropriate are afforded to those representatives";

(d) in section 188(7), at the end insert—

"A failure on the part of the transferor to provide information or other assistance to the transferee does not constitute special circumstances rendering it not reasonably practicable for the transferee to comply with such a requirement.";

(e) where an employment tribunal makes a protective award under section 189 ordering the transferee to pay remuneration for a protected period in respect of a transferring individual, then, so far as the protected period falls before the relevant transfer, the individual's employer before the transfer is to be treated as the employer for the purpose of determining under sections 190(2) to (6) and 191 the period (if any) in respect of which, and the rate at which, the individual is entitled to be paid remuneration by the transferee under section 190(1);

(f) in section 189, at the end insert—

"(7) If on a complaint under this section a question arises whether the transferor agreed to an election or the transferee gave notice of an election as required under section 198A(3), it is for the transferee to show that the agreement or notice was given as required.";

(g) in section 192, at the end insert—

"(5) If on a complaint under this section a question arises whether the transferor agreed to an election or the transferee gave notice of an election as required under section 198A(3), it is for the transferee to show that the agreement or notice was given as required.";

(h) in section 193(6), for "the employer" the second time it appears substitute "the transferor or transferee";

(i) in section 193(7), at the end insert—

"A failure on the part of the transferor to provide information or other assistance to the transferee does not constitute special circumstances rendering it not reasonably practicable for the transferee to comply with any of those requirements.";

(j) in section 196(1), in the closing words, for "employed by the employer" substitute "employed by the transferor or transferee";

(k) or section 196(2) substitute—

"(2) References in this Chapter to representatives of a trade union are to officials or other persons authorised by the trade union to carry on collective bargaining with the transferee.".

(2) Where section 198A applies and the transferee elects to carry out pre-transfer consultation (and has not cancelled the election), both before and after the transfer section 168(1)(c) applies as follows in relation to an official of an independent trade union who, as such an official, is an affected transferring individual's appropriate representative under section 188(1B)(a)—

    (a) in relation to the official's duties as such a representative, the reference in the opening words of section 168(1) to an independent trade union being recognised by the employer is to be read as a reference to an independent trade union being recognised by the transferor;

    (b) the references in section 168(1)(c) to the employer in relation to section 188 are to be read as references to the transferee.".

(2) In section 299 of the Trade Union and Labour Relations (Consolidation) Act 1992 (index of defined expressions)—

    (a) After the entry for "affected employees" insert—

    ""affected transferring individual" (in sections 198A and 198B) | section 198A(7)";

    (b) after the entry for "president" insert—

    ""pre-transfer consultation" (in sections 198A and 198B) | section 198A(7)";

    (c) after the entry for "recognised, recognition and related expressions" insert—

    ""relevant transfer" (in sections 198A and 198B) | section 198A(7)";

    (d) after the entry for "trade union" insert—

    ""transferee" and "transferor" (in sections 198A and 198B) | section 198A(7)

    "transferring individual" (in sections 198A and 198B) | section 198A(7)".

Amendment of the Transfer of Undertakings (Protection of Employment) Regulations 2006

4. The Transfer of Undertakings (Protection of Employment) Regulations 2006 are amended as set out in regulations 5 to 11.

Activities carried out by another person

5.—(1) In regulation 3 (a relevant transfer), after paragraph (2) insert—

"(2A) References in paragraph (1)(b) to activities being carried out instead by another person (including the client) are to activities which are fundamentally the same as the activities carried out by the person who has ceased to carry them out.".

(2) The amendment made by paragraph (1) applies in relation to a TUPE transfer which takes place on or after 31st January 2014.

Restrictions on varying contracts

6.—(1) In regulation 4 (effect of relevant transfer on contracts of employment), for paragraphs (4) and (5) substitute—

"(4) Subject to regulation 9, any purported variation of a contract of employment that is, or will be, transferred by paragraph (1), is void if the sole or principal reason for the variation is the transfer.

(5) Paragraph (4) does not prevent a variation of the contract of employment if—

(a) the sole or principal reason for the variation is an economic, technical, or organisational reason entailing changes in the workforce, provided that the employer and employee agree that variation; or

(b) the terms of that contract permit the employer to make such a variation.

(5A) In paragraph (5), the expression "changes in the workforce" includes a change to the place where employees are employed by the employer to carry on the business of the employer or to carry out work of a particular kind for the employer (and the reference to such a place has the same meaning as in section 139 of the 1996 Act).

(5B) Paragraph (4) does not apply in respect of a variation of the contract of employment in so far as it varies a term or condition incorporated from a collective agreement, provided that—

(a) the variation of the contract takes effect on a date more than one year after the date of the transfer; and

(b) following that variation, the rights and obligations in the employee's contract, when considered together, are no less favourable to the employee than those which applied immediately before the variation.

(5C) Paragraphs (5) and (5B) do not affect any rule of law as to whether a contract of employment is effectively varied.".

(2) The amendment made by paragraph (1) applies in relation to any purported variation of a contract of employment that is transferred by a TUPE transfer if—

(a) the TUPE transfer takes place on or after 31st January 2014, and

(b) that purported variation is agreed on or after 31st January 2014, or, in a case where the variation is not agreed, it starts to have effect on or after that date.

Effect of relevant transfer on contracts of employment which incorporate provisions of collective agreements

7.—(1) After regulation 4, insert—

"**Effect of relevant transfer on contracts of employment which incorporate provisions of collective agreements**

4A.—(1) Where a contract of employment, which is transferred by regulation 4(1), incorporates provisions of collective agreements as may be agreed from time to time, regulation 4(2) does not transfer any rights, powers, duties and liabilities in relation to any provision of a collective agreement if the following conditions are met—

  (a) the provision of the collective agreement is agreed after the date of the transfer; and

  (b) the transferee is not a participant in the collective bargaining for that provision.

(2) For the purposes of regulation 4(1), the contract of employment has effect after the transfer as if it does not incorporate provisions of a collective agreement which meet the conditions in paragraph (1).".

(2) The amendment made by paragraph (1) applies in relation to a TUPE transfer which takes place on or after 31st January 2014.

Dismissal of employee because of relevant transfer

8.—(1) In regulation 7 (dismissal of employee because of relevant transfer), for paragraphs (1) to (3) substitute—

"(1) Where either before or after a relevant transfer, any employee of the transferor or transferee is dismissed, that employee is to be treated for the purposes of Part 10 of the 1996 Act (unfair dismissal) as unfairly dismissed if the sole or principal reason for the dismissal is the transfer.

(2) This paragraph applies where the sole or principal reason for the dismissal is an economic, technical or organisational reason entailing changes in the workforce of either the transferor or the transferee before or after a relevant transfer.

(3) Where paragraph (2) applies—

(a) paragraph (1) does not apply;

(b) without prejudice to the application of section 98(4) of the 1996 Act (test of fair dismissal), for the purposes of sections 98(1) and 135 of that Act (reason for dismissal)—

  (i) the dismissal is regarded as having been for redundancy where section 98(2)(c) of that Act applies; or

(ii) in any other case, the dismissal is regarded as having been for a substantial reason of a kind such as to justify the dismissal of an employee holding the position which that employee held.

(3A) In paragraph (2), the expression "changes in the workforce" includes a change to the place where employees are employed by the employer to carry on the business of the employer or to carry out work of a particular kind for the employer (and the reference to such a place has the same meaning as in section 139 of the 1996 Act).".

(2) The amendment made by paragraph (1) applies in relation to any case where—

(a) the TUPE transfer takes place on or after 31st January 2014, and

(b) the date when any notice of termination is given by an employer or an employee in respect of any dismissal is 31st January 2014 or later, or, in a case where no notice is given, the date on which the termination takes effect is 31st January 2014 or later.

Definition of "permitted variation"

9.—(1) In regulation 9(7) (variations of contract where transferors are subject to relevant insolvency proceedings), for sub-paragraph (a), substitute—

"(a) the sole or principal reason for the variation is the transfer and not a reason referred to in regulation 4(5)(a); and".

(2) The amendment made by paragraph (1) applies in relation to any case where—

(a) the TUPE transfer takes place on or after 31st January 2014, and

(b) the permitted variation is agreed on or after 31st January 2014.

Deadline for notification of employee liability information

10.—(1) In regulation 11(6) (notification of employee liability information), for "fourteen days" substitute "28 days".

(2) The amendment made by paragraph (1) applies in relation to a TUPE transfer which takes place on or after 1st May 2014.

Micro-business's duty to inform and consult where no appropriate representatives

11.—(1) In regulation 13(1) (duty to inform and consult representatives) after "regulations" insert "13A".

(2) After regulation 13 insert—

"Micro-business's duty to inform and consult where no appropriate representatives

13A.—(1) This regulation applies if, at the time when the employer is required to give information under regulation 13(2)—

    (a) the employer employs fewer than 10 employees;

    (b) there are no appropriate representatives within the meaning of regulation 13(3); and

    (c) the employer has not invited any of the affected employees to elect employee representatives.

(2) The employer may comply with regulation 13 by performing any duty which relates to appropriate representatives as if each of the affected employees were an appropriate representative.".

(3) In regulation 15 (failure to inform or consult), in paragraph (3) at the end insert "except where the question is whether or not regulation 13A applied".

(4) In regulation 15 (failure to inform or consult), after paragraph (3) insert—

    "(3A) If on a complaint under paragraph (1), a question arises as to whether or not regulation 13A applied, it is for the employer to show that the conditions in sub-paragraphs (a) and (b) of regulation 13A(1) applied at the time referred to in regulation 13A(1).".

(5) The amendments made by this regulation apply in relation to a TUPE transfer which takes place on or after 31st July 2014.

Jenny Willott

Parliamentary Under Secretary of State for Employment Relations and
Consumer Affairs
8th January 2014
Department for Business, Innovation and Skills

EXPLANATORY NOTE

(This note is not part of the Regulations)

These Regulations relate to the implementation of Council Directive 1998/59/EC on the approximation of the laws of the Member States relating to collective redundancies. They insert new sections into the provisions relating to collective redundancies in the Trade Union and Labour Relations (Consolidation) Act 1992 ("the 1992 Act").

They also relate to the implementation of Council Directive 2001/23/EC ("the 2001 Directive") on the approximation of the laws of the Member States relating to the safeguarding of employees' rights in the event of transfers of undertakings, businesses or parts of undertakings or businesses. The 2001 Directive is implemented in the United Kingdom by the Transfer of Undertakings (Protection of Employment) Regulations 2006 ("the 2006 Regulations"). These Regulations amend the 2006 Regulations in their application in Great Britain. To the extent that they relate to the 2001 Directive they are made under section 2(2) of the European Communities Act 1972. To the extent that they relate to the treatment of employees, and related matters, in relation to a service provision change (in circumstances other than those to which the Directive applies), they are made under section 38 of the Employment Relations Act 1999.

These Regulations extend to Great Britain and not Northern Ireland.

Regulation 3 inserts new sections into the 1992 Act. These sections make provision for a transferee to elect to consult, or start to consult, representatives of affected transferring individuals about the transferee's proposed dismissals before the transfer takes place and set out how sections 188 to 198 of the 1992 Act apply in cases where the transferee has made such an election.

Regulation 5 inserts a new paragraph into regulation 3 of the 2006 Regulations, dealing with the references to "activities" in the definition of a service provision change in regulation 3(1)(b).

Regulation 6 amends the provisions in regulation 4 of the 2006 Regulations concerned with variations to contracts in a situation involving a relevant transfer. Any purported variation of a contract of employment that will be transferred under regulation 4(1) of the 2006 Regulations will be void if the sole or principal reason for the variation is the transfer. However, in certain situations, dealt with in the new paragraphs (5) to (5B), a variation of contract may not be void, though the general rules as to whether a contract is effectively varied continue to apply.

Regulation 9 makes a related amendment to the definition of "permitted variation" in regulation 9 of the 2006 Regulations.

Regulation 7 inserts regulation 4A into the 2006 Regulations, to deal with the effect of a relevant transfer on contracts of employment which incorporate provisions of collective agreements as may be agreed from time to time.

Regulation 8 amends regulation 7 of the 2006 Regulations on the protection against dismissal in situations involving a relevant transfer. If the sole or principal reason for the dismissal of an employee is the transfer, the dismissal is treated as unfair for the purposes of Part 10 of the Employment Rights Act 1996 (unfair dismissal). This does not apply if the sole or principal reason for the dismissal is an economic, technical or organisational reason entailing changes in the workforce of either the transferor or transferee before or after a relevant transfer.

Regulation 10 amends regulation 11 of the 2006 Regulations so that the usual deadline for notification of employee liability information under that regulation is increased from not less than 14 days before the transfer to not less than 28 days before the transfer.

Regulations 11 makes amendments to regulations 13 to 15 of the 2006 Regulations on information and consultation so that a micro-business can inform and consult directly with all the affected employees in cases where there are no existing appropriate representatives.

An impact assessment of the effect that this instrument will have on the costs to business and the voluntary sector and a Transposition Note have been prepared. They are attached to the Explanatory Memorandum which is available alongside the instrument on www.legislation.gov.uk. Copies of these documents have also been placed in the Libraries of both Houses of Parliament.

Index

INDEX

TUPE: LAW & PRACTICE